D1491514

ACC. No: 05205883

The Troubles with Us

The Troubles with Us

One Belfast girl on boys,
bombs and finding her way

Alix O'Neill

4th ESTATE · London

4th Estate
An imprint of HarperCollins*Publishers*
1 London Bridge Street
London SE1 9GF

www.4thEstate.co.uk

HarperCollins*Publishers*
1st Floor, Watermarque Building, Ringsend Road
Dublin 4, Ireland

First published in Great Britain in 2021 by 4th Estate

1

Copyright © Alix O'Neill 2021
Map © Micky O'Neill 2021

Alix O'Neill asserts the moral right to be identified as the author of this work in accordance with the Copyright, Designs and Patents Act 1988

Some names and other features have been changed to protect the privacy of individuals featured in this book.

Quote from 'Mmmbop' by Hanson: Words & Music by Isaac Hanson, Taylor Hanson & Zachary Hanson. © Copyright 1997 Jam 'N' Bread Music; All Rights Administered by Kobalt Music Publishing Limited; All Rights Reserved International Copyright Secured; Used by permission of Hal Leonard Europe Limited.

A catalogue record for this book is available from the British Library

ISBN 978-0-00-839370-0 (hardback)
ISBN 978-0-00-839371-7 (trade paperback)

All rights reserved. No part of this publication may be reproduced, stored in a retrieval system, or transmitted, in any form or by any means, electronic, mechanical, photocopying, recording or otherwise, without the prior permission of the publishers.

This book is sold subject to the condition that it shall not, by way of trade or otherwise, be lent, re-sold, hired out or otherwise circulated without the publisher's prior consent in any form of binding or cover other than that in which it is published and without a similar condition including this condition being imposed on the subsequent purchaser.

Typeset in Bembo by Palimpsest Book Production Ltd, Falkirk, Stirlingshire

Printed and bound in Great Britain by CPI Group (UK) Ltd, Croydon CR0 4YY

MIX
Paper from
responsible sources
FSC
www.fsc.org
FSC® C007454

This book is produced from independently certified FSC™ paper to ensure responsible forest management.

For more information visit: www.harpercollins.co.uk/green

For Daddy D

Hold on to the ones who really care, in the end they'll be the only ones there

Hanson

Contents

Part Two: Them

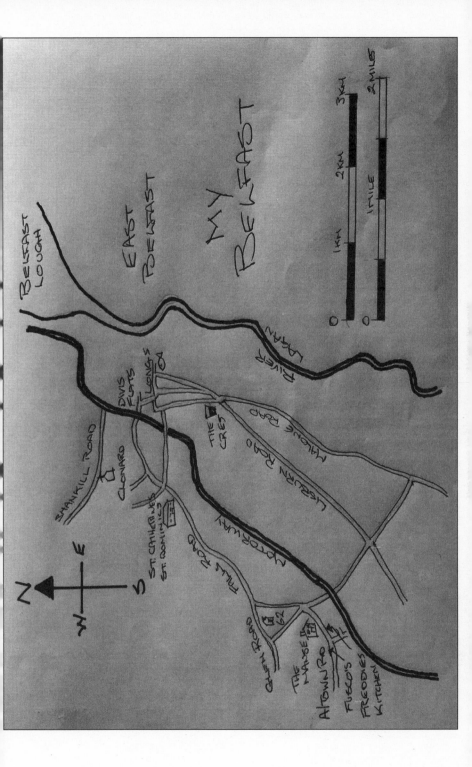

Who's who
(it gets fierce confusing)

My family
Mummy (Anne)
Daddy (Micky)
Toni, my sister

Mummy's ones
*Daddy Devlin (also known as 'Jimmy' – if you're talking
    to a Protestant – or 'Pat' for the Catholics in the room),*
    Mummy's daddy
Mummy Devlin (Mary), Mummy's mummy
Gogi (Tony), Mummy's brother. The eldest in the
    family
John, Mummy's youngest brother
Gerry, Mummy's middle brother
Hil, Mummy's middle sister
Bernie, Mummy's youngest sister
Liz, John's wife
Brendan, Hil's husband

Daddy's ones
Grandma (also Mary), Daddy's mummy
Papa, Daddy's daddy
Roseleen, Grandma's sister
Lily, Grandma's sister
Jacqueline, Daddy's sister
Teresa, Daddy's sister
Ted, Daddy's brother
David, Jacqueline's husband

The Girls
Nat
Mel
Niamh
Jennifer

St Dominic's classmates
Aisling
Colleen
Kelly
Pauline

Boys
Anto, First kiss
Laurie, Teenage obsession
Ryan, Flame-haired dream lover
Yer Man Jamie, Ryan's friend
Sammy, Jennifer's boyfriend
Johnny, Niamh's boyfriend
Dan, University crush
Mr G, Kind of a big deal

The Half-Bloods
Maggie
Liam
Kevin
Erin
Nora

The rest of 'em
Moira, Mummy's best friend
Saoirse, Moira's daughter
Big Sean, Daddy's best friend
Angela, Gogi's girlfriend
Greig, Daddy's friend
Laura, Family friend
Danielle, Best friend at primary school
Podge, Homeless man living at the bottom of our
    garden
Jimmy, Bouncer at the Cres

Author's note

This is a work of creative non-fiction. All the events and people in this story are real, portrayed to the best of my mother's memory and mine. Occasionally, the chronology has been changed, some conversations have been recreated and/or supplemented and I have made two people into one. Some names and identifying details have been changed to protect the privacy of certain individuals (and to avoid my knees being capped).

PART ONE:

US

Prologue

It started with Santa. That was the first whopper in our family. The first I knew about anyway. Most parents have the courtesy to deal their children this devastating blow before they hit adolescence. Or they assume they'll figure it out for themselves.

I was never the kind of kid who figured stuff out.

Mummy should have realised this the day I came home from school, aged nine, and asked whether we were Catholics or Protestants. After five years of being educated by nuns in Belfast, a city where walls were literally built to separate the two.

Still, I have to hand it to the woman, she knew how to do Christmas. On 10 December every year, the day after my sister Toni's birthday, out would come bowls of cinnamon-scented acorns, felt mice dressed as choristers and a hand-knitted tableau of snowmen representing each member of the family. Daddy's been

3

on at her for years to remove his snowman's earring, a painful reminder of his Bono phase.

In the run-up to the big day, Toni and I would find letters from Santa on our bedroom windowsills. He'd praise, in my case, what few scholastic achievements had occurred that year and call out behavioural abnormalities:

> Dear Alix,
> You've been such a good girl this year and I'm pleased you're doing well at school (though Sister Bland has suggested you consider directing plays at break time and not during her maths lessons). However, I'm troubled to hear you've been making your sister wear a loincloth and taking her for walks around the area in a wheelbarrow. This is not on. Please stop, or I'll have to put you on the Naughty List.
> Love ya!
> Santa

It was an effective disciplinary strategy. Any time Mummy invoked one of the Holy Trinity – Santa, the Tooth Fairy and the Easter Bunny – I'd ease up on the ritualistic humiliation of my younger sibling for a few weeks. It wasn't just the threat of a Christmas without presents or a carob-free Easter (because what child doesn't enjoy the caffeine-free and calcium-rich alternative to chocolate?) that kept me in line. You see, as long as Santa and his ilk existed, you got to be a child. You didn't have to deal with grown-up faffs like work and lodging cheques and extracting cocktail sausages from the VHS player (Daddy's yet to see the funny side) – and periods.

When I was 11, Mummy gave me the lowdown on menstruation during the school run.

'Women have a monthly cycle. It's perfectly natural, no need for a fuss. Come to me for sanitary towels. We don't do tampons in this family – they can kill you. Have a great day, love!'

She couldn't understand why people felt the need to talk about basic bodily functions, and so the 'P' word was banned in our house. This was odd, considering the colourful lexicon of profanities that frequently poured out of her mouth – 'ass face' and 'dick features' and 'holy fuck' and – a particular favourite – 'their hole's open', to describe a person of pecuniary meanness.

The real injustice of adulthood, however, was getting old itself. Daddy's mummy spent her retirement on the sofa, saying the rosary and watching daytime TV, while my maternal grandmother died before I was born. As I could see no advantages to the ageing process, I decided not to participate. When friends with older siblings who had cruelly relieved them of their childish notions attempted to enlighten me with the truth about Santa, I refused to listen. Sacrilege! Slander! A pox on your houses!

Yet the evidence was mounting. First, there was the Christmas Eve I caught Daddy putting together the toy petrol station I'd asked for (it was the nineties – oil was sexy). He told me he'd been in the bathroom and had heard a noise. When he went to investigate, he found a half-assembled gas pump by the tree. Assuming he'd scared off Santa, he decided to finish the job for him. The following year, I stumbled across a GeoSafari at the bottom of my uncle Tony's wardrobe while examining his stack of *Playboy*s. As it happened, the interactive educational toy was number one on my Christmas list.

The year I turn twelve the penny finally drops. Or rather, it's hurled right between my eyes with spectacular force. I'm in my second year of an all-girls convent grammar school on the Falls Road. My classmates believe in many things: a united Ireland, a free Palestine and, despite the denouement of their relationship years earlier when she dumped him for Michael Hutchence, the enduring love between Kylie and Jason. They also believe that a man who invites you to sit on his lap and call him Father Christmas is asking for a knee-capping.

It's a Monday in early December. Our form tutor asks us what we got up to over the weekend, so I fill my peers in on our day trip to Lapland. We flew out to Finland on the Saturday morning, went on a reindeer sleigh ride, met the elves, hung out with the big man and were back in time for *Stars in Their Eyes*. I await the sighs of envy. WHACK. A swift, sharp smack across the back of my head. The blow is administered by Aisling, the good-natured hard-ass everyone is keen to get on the right side of.

'Are you wise in the head, wee girl? There is no Santa.'

She starts laughing, her gold hoops bouncing around her cheeks like planetary orbs. The rest of the class join in, but there's no malice in Aisling's teasing. Ever since our mothers met at the school gate on our first day and insisted we walk to assembly together, Aisling has had my back. While we aren't exactly friends, she tolerates my eccentricities and has never threatened to beat me up after school. Which is always nice.

She shuffles towards me now and speaks softly. 'Seriously, Alix, your ma and da buy you presents. Everyone knows that. Just ask them.'

Aisling has always been upfront with me in the past. She was the one to tell me that snacking on scrunched-up pieces of file paper is 'fuckin' weird' and that my attempts to form an appreciation society for the Irish talk show host Gay Byrne were unlikely to succeed.

I decide to bite the bullet later that week at Daddy Devlin's house. (That's Mummy's daddy. We spend every day after school here, so Mummy can make him his tea.) My father is having dinner in front of the news. Something called the Bosnian peace deal has just been signed, which I guess is a big deal, because Daddy doesn't appear to hear me when I spring it on him, the three words I've been dreading to ask.

'What's that, love?' His eyes remain glued to the screen.

'I said, "Does Santa exist?"'

Daddy freezes, a forkful of Findus Crispy Pancake suspended over Slobodan Milošević's head. He puts down his cutlery and starts rooting around the pockets of his jeans for a cigarette. A classic stalling tactic.

'I . . . ummm . . . I'm just going to see if there's any brown sauce. Back in a minute, love.'

The man can't get out the door fast enough. I follow him into the hallway and hover outside the kitchen.

Mummy's at the cooker, attempting to liberate a boil-in-the-bag cod. 'For Christ's sake, Micky, I can't deal with this right now. Where are the scissors?'

She stabs the packet vigorously with a bread knife, parsley butter exploding all over her Benetton jumper. 'Just go back in and tell her of course Santa exists.' Mummy plonks Daddy Devlin's tea in front of him and licks her sleeve. Her father eyes it suspiciously.

'Okay, well, give me some brown sauce then,' says Daddy.

'What?'

'I told her I was off to get brown sauce. If I go back without it, she'll know something's up.'

'There's no brown sauce left, Micky!' Mummy sounding fraught now. 'Here, take some vinegar.'

'Who puts vinegar on a crispy pancake?'

'For fook's sake!' 'Fook' is as close as my grandfather gets to losing his rag. 'Just tell the child, Anne. She's almost a teenager.' His tuppenceworth dispensed, he goes back to sifting through his plate for pieces of buttery plastic.

'Alright, I'll do it. But if you think I'm going in there alone, you can forget it.'

I leg it back into the living room and pretend to be engrossed in the news. Gerry Adams is on now. It's still a novelty hearing the Sinn Féin leader's voice. For years, the British government banned the broadcasting of key members of the party, so every time you'd see Adams on the TV, he was dubbed by an actor. Not that I ever paid much attention to anything the man said. Unlike my peers, I have little interest in the goings-on of the resistance. How could I when there are greater issues at play? Like my parents lying to me my entire life.

Mummy pops her head around the door. 'Have you got a second, love?' Something's up. She's never this conciliatory. 'Your daddy says you were asking about Santa. We need to have a wee talk.'

I. Will. Not. Cry.

'He's not real, is he?'

'Of course he is.'

Daddy elbows Mummy, but stays silent, clearly intent on letting his wife take the hit.

'He's . . . er . . . just more of an idea, a symbol rather than an actual person, y'know? It's what Santa represents that matters – kindness and goodwill and that sort of thing. Isn't that right, Micky?'

'What a load of ballix.' A head of Brylcreemed curls appears behind my dad. It's Uncle Gogi. (It's actually Tony, but my sister, named after her godfather, has been calling him Gogi since she was a baby.) He lights up a Dunhill and sits down beside me, extending a consoling arm around my shoulder. 'Don't worry about it, kiddo. You'll get extra presents this year to make up for it.'

I feel bereft, the victim of fraud, a gross injustice. 'What about the others?' I demand. 'No Tooth Fairy? Easter Bunny? I suppose you're going to tell me lepre-chauns are made up too?'

'Jesus, kid, how have you survived this long?' Gogi stubs out his cigarette, helps himself to the remnants of Daddy's dinner and lights up another fag.

I can't believe it. My whole family is in on it.

I turn to Mummy. Somehow, I know she's the one behind this charade. Closed doors, whispers in the kitchen – my life has been a series of untruths and cover-ups.

'I shall never lie to my children the way you've lied to me.' I say the words slowly and purposefully, being sure to maintain eye contact with my mother throughout. Then I run out of the room, slamming the door behind me. I saw Tamera do this after a row with her dad on *Sister, Sister* and have been waiting for the right moment to inflict some pre-teen angst on my parents.

It took a while to come round, but Gogi was right about the presents. Keen to ensure my silence and hide the awful truth from my sister (turns out she'd copped on long before I did, but didn't want to burst my bubble), Mummy and Daddy went to town that year. Santa managed to find every item of Take That memorabilia in existence, even though Mummy had strong objections to 'those lads in that video with their holes out'.

Christmas was never the same, though. The certainties of childhood were over. Who knew what other horrors lay around the corner? But the Great Santa Conspiracy taught me two important life lessons: being a grown-up can be messy, and parents have secrets too.

1

Beginnings

Here's a crude summary of the Northern Irish situation. There are Catholics and there are Protestants. In theory, we Catholics are big into Mary, Our Lady, the mother of Jesus, She-Who-Gave-Birth-Without-Doing-The-Deed. We like our clergy chaste and our masses short. We swear, we shag and when I was making my confirmation in the early nineties, it was with the utmost sincerity that we took the Pledge – a signed contract with God himself – not to let a single drop of alcohol pass our lips until we were eighteen. I later learnt that most of my friends crossed their fingers behind their backs when reeling off their vow of abstinence and that breaking the Pledge was a rite of passage, any ensuing guilt absolved by a quick confession. Catholics love a bit of confession. It's essentially free therapy that allows you to indulge in all kinds of bad behaviour (including nicking thirty quid out of your husband's wallet when he's passed out drunk and suggesting he lost it in his inebriated stupor – a handy money-saving tip from Mummy). Protestants, on the other hand, prefer their faith without frills, struggle with the whole virgin birth thing and have no need for confession because they make sure they do nothing to feel guilty about in the first place.

Of course, neither side entered into a centuries-old dispute simply over incense and immaculate conception. The faith you were born into, whether you were religious or not, largely dictated your politics. When I was growing up, the majority of Catholics in Northern Ireland wanted to see a united Ireland, while most Protestants were hell-bent on remaining in the UK. Things are less clear-cut these days as the region's post-Troubles generation tends to shun traditional labels. You've got Catholics who are happy with the status quo and Protestants who want reunification, and a big old chunk of the population who identify as neither Protestant nor Catholic, nationalist nor unionist. In short, it's complicated.

But when the Troubles – the thirty-year civil conflict that cost the lives of over three thousand people in the region – kicked off in 1969, it wasn't about belonging; it was about civil rights. Historically, Protestants had all the power. Local government electoral boundaries were drawn to favour unionist candidates, while the right to vote was restricted to ratepayers. As Protestants tended to own businesses and employ their own, Catholics were less likely to have a job, so were politically marginalised.

Northern Ireland is probably the only place where a mixed marriage is a union between two Christians. My grandma took to her bed for a week when Daddy's sister Jacqueline brought home David, a colleague who 'kicked with the other foot'. I don't think her objections were political or even religious (which is pretty much the same thing where I come from) although naturally, she was sceptical of any belief that casts doubt on Our Lady's virtue. She'd seen the fallout from inter-faith marriages – young couples ostracised, families torn apart – and didn't want that for her daughter, oblivious to the fact she was perpetuating the cycle of mistrust.

Daddy went to visit his mother, told her that she hadn't raised them to be prejudiced, and that David was cool – for a Protestant.

A few days later, Auntie Jacqueline called him. 'I don't know what you said to Mummy, but thank you.'

David's parents took longer to come around, refusing to attend the wedding or even acknowledge the birth of their first grandchild.

These days, no one really cares who you sleep with. When it comes to education, however, little has changed – 90-odd per cent of children in the region attend schools that identify with a single tradition.* It wasn't until I moved to London in my mid-twenties that I started to question this segregation. And I often wonder, if I still lived in Belfast, would I send my children to one of its few integrated schools? I'd like to think so, but Northern Ireland is a funny place. Old prejudices die hard.

For all our faults, we're a friendly bunch. Visit any restaurant and you'll be invited to take a 'wee seat', have a 'wee look at the menu there' and when you're

---

* According to government figures.

done, 'enter your wee PIN' into the card machine. So much more than a linguistic tic, 'wee' softens blows, it tells the person you're addressing you're concerned for their comfort, makes the unpleasant palatable. 'Now I'm just going to insert this speculum into your wee vagina and that's your wee smear all done, alright?'

There were lots of wee bombs during my childhood. Like the coffee jar stuffed with Semtex and shrapnel that was abandoned in our garden by a rogue 'RA man as he was legging it from the police. It's all good – we weren't the targets of this inept attempt at terrorism. The would-be aggressor had intended on chucking the device at the Brits, and our front garden, about 10 feet above road level, provided the perfect vantage point for a surprise attack. Unfortunately for the chap in question, he was spotted by a soldier on foot patrol and had to abort his mission, escaping out the back of the house and leaving his handiwork in my mother's prized rose bush.

We were heading back from Daddy Devlin's when we saw our road cordoned off by the police. An officer told Mummy they were investigating a 'situation'. (FYI, everything is a situation in Northern Ireland.) It was hours before we were allowed back home, not that Mummy was fazed. She parked the car outside Freddie's Kitchen across the street and let us have sweet and sour chicken balls for tea while she caught up on the latest issue of *Woman's Own*. A win for everyone.

I should probably explain, I spent the first eighteen years of my life on the Falls Road. Yep, *that* Falls Road.

The one with the balaclava-ed youths you used to see on the six o'clock news hurling petrol bombs and guldering,* 'Fuck off back home, ye British bastards!' So really, the odd coffee-jar bomb wasn't anything to get exercised about.

That. That last sentence, that casual dismissal of finding a *bomb* in your back garden as though it were perfectly normal – this is the result of spending your formative years in Belfast. It's only now, at the grand old age of thirty-six, two children and three geographical moves later, that I'm starting to get it. How my childhood was anything but normal.

The Falls runs from Divis Street, in the city centre, to Andersonstown (or Andytown as the locals call it), in the suburbs of west Belfast. You might have heard of Divis Tower, back when Belfast dominated the headlines. Built in the 1960s, the 200-foot-tall concrete monolith housed not just working-class Catholics, but the British Army, who took over the top two floors as an observation post, accessible only by helicopter.

When the violence first erupted in 1969, nine-year-old Patrick Rooney became the first child to die in the Troubles after the Royal Ulster Constabulary, claiming it was coming under sniper attack from the tower, opened fire on the flats. (Nationalists generally regarded the RUC – now the more inclusively named

---

* Northern Irish for 'a loud shout', according to Oxford Languages, 'typically as an expression of anger'. There's a lot of guldering where I come from.

Police Service of Northern Ireland – as an occupying force, a Protestant police for a Protestant people, in bed with the Brits. Up to a third of places in the force were initially reserved for Catholics, but in 1993 the take-up rate stood at just 7 per cent. According to the RUC, this figure rose to 25 per cent during the two IRA ceasefires in the years that followed.)

I went to school, primary and secondary, a short drive from Divis Tower, and if you headed further up the Falls to Andytown, you'd reach our house. From the age of seven, I lived with my family in an old manse that used to belong to the Presbyterian church when the area was nothing but countryside. As Belfast expanded and Catholics started moving in, the Prods cleared out and had long gone by the time my grandparents arrived from the Lower Falls, when Mummy was sixteen. Andytown was, and still is, staunchly republican.

We bought the house off Daddy Devlin when he upped sticks for the salubrious Malone Road with Gogi and Mummy's youngest brother, John. The relocation was unfortunate for my sister and me. To our peers, west was best, full stop. You didn't aspire to a less segregated existence no matter how well you'd done for yourself. No, a BT9 postcode meant only one thing – 'snobby bastard'. In leafy south Belfast, there were no flags hanging from the lampposts, no pavement kerbs painted green, white and orange or red, white and blue. Monied Catholics were too preoccupied with their delis and their horse-riding lessons to bother about living next door to the other side. And Protestants knew any *taig* lucky enough to migrate south was unlikely to get all *tiocfaidh ár lá*★ on them.

Even if my granddad had stayed local, we were snobby bastards anyway for living in a big house. Not that that was necessarily a bad thing. It was just a fact. Like the fact Protestants had cleaner shoes and covered their toasters in clingfilm. (It solved the crumbs problem.)

The Manse was a far cry from Mummy's childhood home. She spent her early years in a two-up two-down with an outside toilet on Durham Street, at the bottom of the Falls. My maternal granny, Mary or 'Mummy Devlin', God rest her (an expression I've picked up from my mother when referencing the dearly departed), scrubbed Mummy and her brothers once a week in a tin tub in front of the fire. They lived with Mummy Devlin's blind mother, who was hooked on snuff. She used to keep a bag of coins under her pillow and ask Mummy to buy her a cone full of the ground tobacco leaves, giving her a ha'penny for her troubles. Mummy always spoke fondly of this period of her life. I think it was her happiest time. Before things got a bit mad.

Mummy Devlin had no time for gossips – and people frequently gossiped about our family – or prying into the lives of others. My mother once asked a pregnant neighbour on the bus when she was due. When they got home, Mummy Devlin smacked her across the back of the head with a leather glove over the intrusion. She was twenty-one at the time.

★ *Tiocfaidh ár lá* is a republican slogan. The translation is: Our day will come.

My childhood was accompanied by a soundtrack of Mummy Devlin-isms, arcane expressions Mummy insisted were in common usage in her mother's day: 'he was dressed to the air of Willy Riley' (he looked smart); 'that Áine has a quare leg for a button boot' (Áine has slim calves); 'I'm like an eatin' house detective' (I'm starving); and 'yer man Liam isn't worth the full of his arse roasted snow' ('I don't have a great deal of time for that Liam fellow'). I've yet to find a single soul who can verify this last bizarre locution, but Mummy couldn't give a 'fiddler's fart' what anyone else says. The only saying that made any kind of sense was, 'Are they putting bread on your table?' a retort to those who felt compelled to interfere in our business. *Never explain, never apologise* – my mother has lived her life by these words.

Mummy Devlin took her daughter everywhere with her – to mass, bowling, more mass. She also encouraged her to go places by herself, live a little. Which is how Mummy ended up alone one Friday night at the hottest ticket in town, *The Song of Bernadette*, a local parish production about the apparition of the Virgin Mary to a teenage girl in Lourdes. The lead must have given a convincing performance: when Mummy got home that night to an empty house, she switched on all the lights and frantically checked under the beds for any sign of Herself. My grandfather found her two hours later standing on top of the Ercol two-seater.

'What are you doing up there?' he demanded.

'I'm afraid Our Lady is going to appear to me from under the sofa.'

'Anne, if Our Lady should come to Belfast, you're the last person she'll appear to. Now get down from there.'

Occasionally, she was persuaded by friends to engage in regular teenage activities. It was at her school's sixth form dance that she met my father. He was dating Prudence, the glamorous daughter of an eminent Catholic heart surgeon from the Malone Road. (Snobby bastard, obviously.) Sadly, Mummy's plus one was less in demand – years later, it emerged he was a paedophile. But the minute Daddy set eyes on my mum, it was game over for poor Prudence. Untameable eyebrows and a face defiantly bare of make-up, the 5-foot-1¾ (the ¾ is crucial) ball of energy on the dance floor was the girl he had to be with.

It was an unexpected match. Mummy was captain of her house, and hockey goalkeeper. She didn't drink or smoke, and went to civil rights marches on her own. 'She was different like that,' Daddy told me when I asked him what life was like in the dark ages. 'She would open doors for me – she never let me be the man – and if she didn't get her own way, she'd stop in the middle of the street and press her nose up against a wall. I was scundered* all the time by her, but she was like no girl I'd ever met, and I loved that about her. Plus, she was hot.'

Daddy, meanwhile, was all fags and flares, and had zero interest in academia. He went to art college, the first in his family to make it to higher education. Any parental pride soon evaporated, however, when he was

---

* Belfast for 'mortified'. Not to be confused with 'scunnered', Ballymena-speak for 'bummed out'.

arrested in Florence for trying to steal a Vespa. Mummy was due to pick him up from the bus station on the Saturday, but Daddy was a no-show.

The following day, she got a call from her new boyfriend's father. Sitting on the stairs in the hallway of the Manse, nervously wrapping the phone's curly cord around her finger, Mummy asked after my grandma and made sure to mention she was just back in from mass.

But my grandfather was in no mood for pleasantries. 'Hello, my dear. I believe you were waiting to pick my son up last night? Well, you'd have been waiting a long time. He's in jail.'

For all his bad-boy antics, Daddy was resolutely against sex before marriage, much to Mummy's horror.

'Let me tell you, it wasn't for want of trying on my part,' she told me recently, apropos of nothing, in the middle of the M&S Foodhall on Donegall Place. 'We went to London for a weekend when we were stepping out back in the seventies. I pushed the single beds together, but your father was having none of it.'

Daddy lived around the corner from Mummy in an ever-changing arrangement in a small three-bedroom semi. There were his parents, brother, four sisters, two aunts and paternal grandmother, Big Granny. (Ironically, they hadn't enough room for Wee Granny.) At one stage, Daddy and my uncle Ted shared a single bed in their parents' room, the grandmother and aunts cosied up and Daddy's sisters had the box room. Big Granny died before Daddy started going out with Mummy, considerably freeing up some space.

Whenever Mummy would call round in the evenings, she'd have to wait in the kitchen while the family finished the rosary. They couldn't go into town to socialise. It was too dangerous to leave the area, especially for young Catholic men, who were likely to be picked up by the soldiers.

The early 1970s were the worst years of the Troubles, when my parents' generation was coming of age. Mummy, Daddy and their friends were around at the very beginning, witnessed the precise moment the shit hit the fan. I remember Daddy telling us about waiting for his best friend Big Sean to pick him up for mass when he was fifteen. It was 15 August 1969, the Feast of the Assumption. Days earlier, violence broke out in Derry between the RUC and the Catholic residents of the Bogside area. It was the first time in UK history that police fired tear gas at rioters. In support of the Bogsiders, nationalists across Northern Ireland held protests. Loyalists responded by attacking Catholic districts. Homes and businesses were burnt out, hundreds of Catholic families driven from their homes and seven people killed.

As Daddy looked out the window of his living room, he saw his friend on the back of a flatbed truck heading in the opposite direction from the chapel. He was coming back from his Aunt Sissy's. Her house had been petrol bombed by loyalists from the Shankill* and Big Sean and his sister Maureen were moving Sissy and

---

* One of the main roads leading through west Belfast, the Shankill is as staunchly loyalist as the Falls is nationalist.

her belongings to safety. Daddy jumped on the back of the lorry to help, joining a caravan of trucks piled high with armchairs, statues of Our Lady and reproduction gilt-framed photos of JFK (almost as much of a pin-up as the Sacred Heart) as they made their way up the Falls past piles of smouldering rubble.

Days later, the British government launched Operation Banner, sending troops to Northern Ireland as a temporary fix to restore order. Peace lines, a series of walls separating Protestant and Catholic communities in interface areas, were built, and women, my grandmothers included, welcomed the soldiers with open arms and steaming mugs of tea. Even Gogi, coming home from the pub, would invite the boys in for a nightcap.

The Army maintained its hero status among Catholics until the Falls Curfew in 1970. My parents had just started going out when soldiers began searching the area for weapons and members of the IRA. Some kids threw stones and petrol bombs, and in response, the British released tear gas and sealed off homes as they put residents on a thirty-six-hour curfew. Four civilians died, seventy-eight were wounded. It was a turning point in the relationship, the moment Catholics lost faith in those who were meant to protect them. You didn't dare so much as smile in a soldier's direction after that, Mummy said. She'd gone to school with a girl who was punished by the IRA for 'fraternising with the enemy'; her head was shaved and she was tarred, feathered and tied to a lamppost.

I remember Daddy telling us that in the weeks and

months following the Falls Curfew, the IRA had no shortage of eager new recruits, though not everyone had the nous required to excel at the terrorism game.

'To make a pipe bomb, right, you need a vice to squeeze the end of the pipe,' he said, settling back into his chair. 'This will keep it nice and tight. First, you drill a hole in the middle where the fuse will go, then you're ready to stuff it with your explosive mixture. In those days, it was fertiliser and sugar.

'Anyway, Jim Davey – he lived down the road from us – he didn't have a vice, you see. So he hammered one end flat, threw in the explosives, then started beatin' away at the other end. Lost a couple of fingers, the buck eejit.'

(At this juncture in the story, I feel it necessary to stress that for all my father's talk of manning the barricades, Grandma would have taken her slipper – the Irish mother's weapon of choice – to his backside had he come home a minute past 9 p.m. The closest he got to joining the revolution was writing 'Up the 'RA' on a wet cement wall during a daytrip to Portaferry.)

Daddy asked Mummy to marry him three times. But Mummy Devlin was ill. The doctor kept telling her she was fine, that it was all in her head. By the time they knew it was ovarian cancer, it was too late. Mummy quit her job as a primary school teacher to nurse her mother.

Despite his previous delinquencies, Daddy had grown on my grandmother and she encouraged Mummy to accept his proposal. One of the last things she did was buy her daughter her wedding dress, knowing she'd never see her in it. Mummy Devlin died at home on 23 December 1979. The next day, Christmas Eve, Mummy got up early. She glazed a ham and decorated the tree. Then she buried her mother. My parents got married the following year.

They moved five minutes away to the Glen Road – Mummy couldn't go far with four younger siblings and Daddy Devlin to look after – and bought twenty-four chickens, two goats (Seamus and Elizabeth: the great Irish poet and the reigning monarch – how's that for bridging the divide?) and a sweet shop, which they named after their sheepdog, Basil.

Mummy briefly considered going back into teaching, but decided it wasn't for her. When she was at school, there were only three career options for a woman – you could be a nurse, a nun or a teacher. No one mentioned making a living selling brandy balls. When the shop on Amelia Street came up for sale, she jumped at the chance, taking over the day-to-day running of the business while Daddy joined an ad agency as a graphic designer. It was his first professional role after a series of odd jobs since the age of fourteen – he'd been a postman, a painter and decorator and a banana packer at the Fyffes factory down the docks.

It was a little slice of the good life – the sweets and the grown-up job and the animal husbandry. Until dogs from the neighbouring estate ate half the chickens, and rats preyed on the eggs of the remaining girls. Daddy would beat them away with a hurling stick, etching a new notch for every rodent taken out.

The goats fared better, benefiting from daily exercise.

Once, my mother was going to vote in the local elections and decided to bring Seamus along for the walk. She tied a rope around his neck and made Auntie Bernie, her youngest sister, wait outside the polling station at St Teresa's with him. Bernie still hasn't forgiven her.

My parents raised turkeys one year, slaughtered by a local butcher in the run-up to Christmas and left to hang in the garage for ten days before collection. They kept two alive for Easter, in case anyone fancied a break from lamb. A few days before Christmas, these remaining two turkeys were stolen. Determined the thieves wouldn't gain from their roguery, Mummy called the Pamela Ballantine show on Downtown Radio. She told Pamela that the reason the birds were still alive was because they were suspected of having a rare form of dysentery and that she and Daddy were waiting on the Department of Agriculture to get back to them with the results. Daddy was in the car on his way to work, listening to the show.

'Now as you all know, we stopped the lost pets slot a while ago,' said Pamela over the airwaves. 'But I'm making an exception on this occasion. Two turkeys have been stolen from a house in west Belfast.'

My father's eyebrows shot up. He steadied his grip on the steering wheel and turned up the volume.

'You may ask yourselves, listeners, why the turkeys were still alive this close to Christmas. Let me tell you – it's because they're *diseased*. And to whoever took them and eats them, I hope you get what you deserve.'

Mummy says the arse fell clean out of the black market for turkeys that year.

When she found out she was pregnant three years later, Mummy knew she wanted to have me at home. Everyone objected. Her male GP told her to, 'Go home and think about it, dear. You'll soon come to your senses'. Grandma was horrified. If breastfeeding was considered transgressive in 1980s Belfast, home births were practically unheard of. Mummy found the only transcendental meditation teacher in town to equip her with the mental resilience to 'ride the crest of the wave' and when the time came, she was ready.

The Glorious Twelfth, when Protestants celebrate the victory of 'King Billy' (William of Orange if you want to be official about it) over Catholic King James in the Battle of the Boyne, isn't a great time to go into labour if you're a Catholic. We get all riled up by the flutes and the drums of the Orange parades, and the papal effigies burning on top of bonfires, and respond by chucking petrol bombs at the authorities. Aside from the violence, everywhere is shut, and the places that do stay open are like graveyards. For those not inclined to march or get themselves arrested, Belfast on the twelfth of July is zero craic.

Luckily, I arrived on my due date, 14 July 1983. Daddy took the placenta down the back of the garden and set it alight. He had a Harp shandy and a cigarette with the midwife, locked the door when she left and climbed into bed beside his wife and baby daughter. They stayed there for two days. A rather glorious fourteenth.

2

Five go bus-burning

'Alix the ballix – did yer ma and da want boys? Hahaha!'

I used to curse my parents for the names they'd given us. Alix and Toni were always going to stand out in a classroom full of Bronaghs and Siobháns. But Mummy assures me it was a calculated decision to avoid future discrimination. When her father Patrick James started his bookmaking business in the 1950s, he became known as 'Jimmy'. Only Mummy Devlin continued to call him Pat. That was how working-class Catholics got ahead then – you had to not be a working-class Catholic. Later, I discovered I'd been called Alix on a whim. My parents had settled on Victoria, and Mummy has a card in the attic from Grandma welcoming baby Vicky to the world, but when Daddy went to the hospital to return the gas and air, he started flicking through a copy of *The Sun* in reception and saw an article by a journalist named Alix Palmer. 'I'd like to call her Alix,' he told Mummy when he got home, and Mummy had no objections. (Though Daddy maintains it was the *Daily Mirror* he'd been reading – he wouldn't use 'that Tory rag to wipe me arse with'.)

There were benefits to the gender-neutral approach. We never had to bother with Prod names when we went to the leisure centre on the Shore Road, for example. (Protestants had the best swimming pools.) Unlike my cousin Oisín the time we went to practise our breaststroke with Uncle Brendan, who was married to Mummy's sister Hil. He made us call Oisín, the son of Mummy's other sister Bernie (you'll get the hang of us) 'Billy', the most Protestant name going. Followed closely by my former alias, Victoria. (Nothing is straight-forward in my family.) It was unfortunate Oisín had a thick mop of flaming red hair – everyone knew Fenians were, like, 80 per cent more likely to carry the ginger gene – but no working-class Catholic in their right mind would have called their son William, so we could enjoy our pool time in peace.

Oisín was only five or six, relatively young to process the complexity of tribal politics, but he accepted his dual identity without question. It was normal to have a fake name in your back pocket should you find yourself in unfamiliar company. Just as it was normal to encounter soldiers squatting outside your driveway and patrolling your street corner. I saw guns every day of my life. It didn't bother me. They were our reality, the only reality we knew. What's the line in Baz Luhrmann's 'Everybody's Free (To Wear Sunscreen)', the one about life's inalienable truths? *Prices will rise, politicians will philander, you too will get old.* If you grew up in Belfast during the Troubles, semi-automatics were simply another inalienable truth.

At a family wedding a few years ago, my sister shared

an anecdote with some non-Northern Irish guests about the time bullets shattered the window of her classroom during an after-school music lesson. She's not sure exactly how old she was, probably eight or nine, or the specific details, but she distinctly recalls her teacher telling the children to take cover under the desks.

'I don't remember that,' said Mummy.

'How can you not? Mrs Heaney told you I was shaken up by the whole thing and you said I'd get over it.'

Mummy shrugged and took a sip of her pinot grigio. 'It does sound like something I'd say. Sure that kind of thing happened all the time.'

'Oh aye, we were always ducking and diving,' Daddy chimed in. 'I'd be walking home from art college with my portfolio like a big ponce, buses on fire all round me.'

The bus-burning was a pain alright. In my parents' day they stopped coming up the Falls because the locals would set them alight and use them as barricades to keep the Army out. I got detention once for being late when we had to take a diverted route thanks to the carcass of a 10A blocking the road. You'd think the teachers would have been more understanding. It's not everywhere that 'Sorry, Miss, it was the war' is a legitimate excuse for tardiness. All things considered, I got off lightly. My friend's uncle knew a taxi driver who was on a job near Cupar Street, off the Falls, while residents were firing rocks and explosives at the police from behind a charred bus. He saw a local alcoholic watching on, swigging from a bottle of wine and smoking a cigarette. One of the protestors handed the unfortunate a petrol bomb and told him to get involved, only he threw his wine by mistake and drank the petrol bomb, his fag sending him up in flames. The protestors jumped on him to put the fire out, breaking his ribs in the process. 'Talk about having a bad day,' the taxi driver chuckled.

Guns and self-immolation aside, my childhood was a halcyon period of Enid Blyton books and summers by the sea in Connemara, on Ireland's west coast. Mummy enrolled Toni and me in a host of after-school activities: piano lessons (I was dismissed by the teacher for lacking 'the slightest hint of musicality'); the YMCA kids' club (kicked out for 'language at odds with the organisation's Christian values') and circus school. It was here, as a stilt walker, I found my calling. The conflict on our doorstep never penetrated this bubble of childhood bliss my mother had so carefully constructed for us.

I can't say the same for kids living in Monaghan and Cavan, just over the border in the Republic. According to friends who grew up there, a popular game back in the nineties was 'IRA'. You had two teams, each with a code word, but each team member knew only one letter. The idea was to capture members of the opposing team and extract the letters from them by any means necessary. The worst beatings were reserved for a recovered teammate you suspected of having talked. They were an unhinged lot, those southerners.

The only time in those early years I saw my parents

ruffled by life outside of our bubble was the Mother's Day we took my father's parents to Newcastle. We'd booked Sunday lunch at a smart restaurant and everyone was looking forward to a day out. On a back road outside Lisburn, we ran into traffic. Daddy didn't realise there was an Army checkpoint just ahead, and moved into the outside lane. He was pulled over and asked for ID. A soldier took his licence to the back of the Land Rover in front of us to run Daddy's details.

He kept us for almost an hour, allowing other cars through, my father getting increasingly worked up, Grandma wanting to turn back in case things turned ugly. (During that period in Northern Ireland, minor incidents could escalate quickly.) Eventually, the soldier said we could go on, smirking as he handed Daddy back his licence.

We weren't sure if it was our address the soldier had an issue with (you don't find many unionists on the Falls) or maybe he thought we were trying to skip the traffic, and wanted to teach Daddy a lesson. Either way, none of us had much of an appetite for our roast lamb that day.

It wasn't all bad living in a war zone. When the much-loved toy store LeisureWorld was bombed in October 1991, the subsequent fire sale provided the perfect opportunity for parents to snap up some serious bargains in time for Christmas. And when Daddy's friend Declan's nose was broken after he was headbutted on a night out (the guy said Declan had been trying to steal his taxi) the silver lining was considerable. Relating the story to a solicitor friend, Declan said his aggressor had added insult to injury by calling him a 'specky bastard'.

'You mean a "specky *Fenian* bastard?"' the solicitor replied. And just like that, one specky Fenian bastard got an eight-grand payday.

3

The man who hid

'What's the craic with your grandda?'

I'm nine years old. My friend Gráinne is lying next to me on the grass, rubbing sun cream over freckled limbs. We were close in primary school, but grew apart as we got older. The last I heard she was serving time for robbing a travel agent's.

'What do you mean?'

My grandfather appears on the doorstep, bare-chested, his navy cords rolled up to his knees. He's wrapped a shirt, turban-style, around his head; his hair is starting to thin, save for a thick wisp of silver skimming an aquiline nose. The man is obsessed with getting his daily dose of vitamin D. Daddy Devlin nods at us as he walks past, chewing on a clove of garlic. (He refused to see a doctor about his hypertension as he didn't want to go on tablets. Every day, Mummy would take his blood pressure with a sphygmomanometer. It's a source of great pride that her daughters had a sound grasp of medical nomenclature by the time we were six and four. 'Say it and spell it, girls,' she'd say.

'*Gyn-ae-col-ogy*'.) He sits on his bench, his head buried in *The 120 Days of Sodom*. He reads everything – Dickens, Poe, Jilly Cooper. Cosmology tomes and textbooks on Esperanto. Travel guides to places he'll never go.

What's the craic with your grandda?

I knew from a young age Daddy Devlin wasn't like other grandparents. Not the sit-on-my-knee-and-tell-me-about-your-day kind. He didn't magic toffees from behind your ear or pretend to steal your nose with his thumb and forefinger. His grandfatherly gift was his knowledge and he bestowed this generously, whether you sought it or not. One of his greatest pleasures was chess. He had boards set up all around the house, his opponents eastern Europeans, who he found in the classified pages of *Chess* magazine and played with remotely. A game could take years as he waited for the next move to arrive in the post. Daddy Devlin didn't mind. He had all the time in the world.

I spent countless evenings at the mahogany rolltop writing desk in my grandfather's study, every inch of the floor covered in newspapers and books annotated in Quink. Daddy Devlin's Jack Russell, Moses, and Staffordshire bull terrier, Rambo, sat by his feet as I attempted to get to grips with the rudiments of algebra or German. If you drifted off during a lesson, he'd jab you in the side with a bony elbow. When really frustrated, he'd drop the F bomb: 'Quit fooking around, child, and pay attention!' I admired his restraint. No one else in the family bothered to check their language around us. Midway through a meal out with Gogi when I was five, Mummy had to take Toni and me aside to explain that 'hard as fuck' is not an acceptable response to 'How was your baked potato, Sir?'

Aside from our trips to Connemara, a wild and remote part of County Galway, Daddy Devlin rarely left the house. He bought the Connemara cottage in the early nineties, back when sheep and potholes ruled Ireland's highways. I once saw 'Are you having a laugh?' furiously daubed across a bumpy stretch of asphalt in red paint. More than a billion in EU funding later and once you reach Dublin, the N6 will get you to Galway in no time. We had no such luxuries then, easily spending seven or eight hours on the road, crawling past fields of turf in the pitch black to get to our destination.

One time, Auntie Hil called Mummy at 8 p.m., asking if she fancied heading to Connemara for the weekend. An hour later, Mummy screeched to a halt outside Hil's, who ushered our cousins into the back seat with Toni and me, the four of us half-asleep and in our pyjamas. We arrived at the house at 5 a.m., coming back two days later for school. For Mummy, the inconvenience was a small price to pay for sea air and the absence of other people.

We were convinced our mother had inherited Daddy Devlin's reclusive streak. Any time the doorbell rang, she made us hide under the console table in the hallway. It didn't matter who it was – we had to get on all fours and take cover. I have a vivid memory of Mummy's schoolfriend Moira, her nose pressed up against the frosted glass panel in the front door.

'Anne?'

Mummy ssh-ed us.

'Anne, I can see you and the girls under the table.'

Mummy brazened it out, casually dusting off her tracksuit bottoms as she emerged from her hideout. 'Oh, hi! Didn't see you there, girl. We were just doing a bit of cleaning.'

Moira bought none of it. But she'd been friends with my mother long enough not to expect an explanation.

My years of crouching beneath that console table gave me an arse of steel – and a suspicion of unexpected visitors. To this day, whenever the doorbell rings, my natural instinct is to duck behind the sofa. Although there's no guarantee I wouldn't be rumbled.

Not long after Mummy and Daddy got married, my father's parents turned up unannounced. Mummy was at home with Bernie and Hil. Panicking she didn't have so much as a teabag in the house, never mind a packet of Rich Tea, to offer her new in-laws, Mummy pulled her sisters down beside her behind the settee, but they were spotted by Grandma.

Mummy pretended they'd been playing hide-and-seek, and answered the door, offering them a cuppa. As my grandparents sat in the living room, she got Hil and Bernie to sift through the wheelie bin out the back for used teabags. Papa said it was the best cup of tea he'd ever had.

I once asked Daddy, 'Why all the drama with Mummy's ones?' Did Daddy Devlin demand this one-woman security detail or did Mummy encourage his eccentricities?

'Chicken or egg, you mean?' Daddy said, rolling his eyes. 'They're both as odd as each other.'

Whatever triggered my grandfather's wariness of others, being robbed at gunpoint in his own house likely made him less inclined to reach out to his neighbours. It was 1971, the year loyalist paramilitary group the Ulster Volunteer Force blew up a Catholic-owned pub, killing fifteen, the IRA exploded a bomb outside a furniture showroom – four people died, including two babies – and the British Army arrested and imprisoned 342 people without trial.

Daddy Devlin was at home in the Manse with Uncle John, then six, when a gang of armed men burst through the back door. They tied my grandfather to a chair, demanding rifles and cash. When he didn't respond, one of the men hit him across the head with a gun. John told them there was money in the safe. The Manse was full of safes, hidden behind reproduction Constables and van Eycks, stashed beneath beds, where proceeds from the family bookmaking business were deposited at the end of each day. Eventually the men left, their pockets stuffed with banknotes retrieved from a secret cabinet tucked behind *The Hay Wain*, my grandfather still bound to his chair.

Afterwards, Daddy Devlin installed metal grilles across the windows at the back of the house, blocking out what little natural light remained. Old horse chestnut trees lined the yard leading off the kitchen, up to the back garden, their branches intertwining to form a leafy canopy. Beneath the surface, the trees had taken hold of the old plumbing system. Builders had to dig up the pipes to remove the roots that had coiled around the water tubes and forced their way into the cracks.

Mummy told me about Daddy Devlin and John and the gunmen over breakfast when I was a teenager. It was a throwaway anecdote, bookended by instructions to quit messing around with my Bran Flakes and do my best not to piss off Sister Malachy during Geography.

She had a knack for that, lumping together the extraordinary and the mundane. On a family trip to London a few years ago, she gestured at Brixton Prison as we walked past. 'I was there once.'

'What? When?'

'Ah, years ago. I was visiting the London bomber.'

'Sorry, can you repeat that?' I stopped in the middle of the street.

Mummy Devlin had been good friends with a woman named Kathleen, who owned a pub in the Shankill area. Kathleen was into pencil skirts and not lighting her own cigarettes. Mummy didn't know Kathleen's eldest son Michael all that well – he was a couple of years older than Mummy and a quiet, unassuming sort. One day, Kathleen and her daughter Sarah arrived at the house, tears rolling down Kathleen's cheeks.

'Oh Mary!' she sobbed, handing my grandmother her coat. 'Michael has been arrested, but he had nothing to do with that bomb.'

'That bomb' was the IRA car bombing of the Old Bailey on 8 March 1973, injuring 200 people. Ten were arrested, among them sisters Dolours and Marian Price, and Kathleen's Michael.

'I'm beside myself, Mary,' said Kathleen, attempting to open a silver cigarette case with unsteady fingers. 'Sarah, light me a cigarette!'

Mummy Devlin instructed Mummy to fetch Kathleen a cup of tea. When they left, Mummy asked her mother if she thought Michael had done it.

'Wash those cups for me,' Mummy Devlin said, sighing.

Honouring her friendship with Kathleen, my grandmother made up a care package of toiletries, and when, months later, Mummy was packing for a trip to London to take part in a national debating competition – she'd already won the regional round – Mummy Devlin told her to visit Michael in Brixton Prison. The guard greeted the twenty-year-old Irish girl with a grunt and asked her to open the parcel. Holding up a bar of Imperial Leather to the light, he sniffed the soap suspiciously before cutting it in half with a penknife and sending Mummy on her way. Michael was released thirteen years later.

I'd say Daddy Devlin turned to mindfulness or yoga to process his ordeal with the gunmen. The man spent most Sundays in downward dog while Mummy Devlin was at mass. He had no time for the church. After his father died when he was twelve, his mother took in lodgers to make ends meet. When one of them passed away, he left her some money. It was a small amount, but enough to make a difference. While her son was at work, she had a visit from the parish priest. He'd heard about her situation and felt it his Christian duty to drop by. He was worried she'd be taken advantage of, that she wouldn't know what to do with the money.

Best leave that burden to the church. From that day on, Daddy Devlin was done with men in dog collars telling him how to live his life.

For all of my grandfather's idiosyncrasies, he had an acute sense of fairness – an Atticus Finch in Boo Radley's skin. On the rare occasions he received visitors, he'd offer advice and money if needed, no strings attached, no judgement. Not that we appreciated these qualities. We enjoyed our grandfather in his less didactic moments. Every Christmas Eve, we'd set off for a long walk in the woods near his house, carrying torches and flasks of honeyed tea, Rambo and Moses tearing ahead, Daddy Devlin making up ghost stories. He came alive at night with no one around to bother him.

Education was everything to him and he offered no apologies for sticking his Roman nose into ours. Self-taught, he left school at fourteen to support his mother and sister, doing various odd jobs until 1953, when he'd made enough money to purchase a small pub on the Old Lodge Road. He worked fifteen hours a day, seven days a week. When the bookie next door got into financial trouble, he bought the business off him and teamed up with Roy, a Protestant engineer, who'd recently returned from Canada with money to invest. As a Catholic sole trader, Daddy Devlin was restricted to working in certain areas of the city. Joining forces with Roy allowed him to expand the business. By 1985, he had seven betting shops and two pubs.

I was raised there, on those betting shop floors, behind those bars. Anytime we were in town with Mummy, we'd pop in to see Gogi in the head office above the bookie's — my uncle was in charge of the day-to-day running of the business by the time I came along. The place would be thick with smoke — everyone had a fag in one hand and a calculator in the other — but it was strangely peaceful, nothing but the murmur of racing commentators on the TV and the thumbing of dockets with rubber thimbles. We'd run to hug Daddy Devlin's cousin Jim, a timid man with a shock of white hair, then jump on Maura's knee. A middle-aged woman with plasters around her thumbs from paper cuts and sovereign rings on her fingers, like Jim, she'd been working for my grandfather for years.

In the pub downstairs, we'd read our books in the snug beside the bar while Mummy chatted to the regulars, who, in between pints, nipped into the shop next door to place their bets. They'd come back, heads shaking, saying the next race would be their race. When I was at university I worked in the bookie's for a couple of weeks every summer. I'd watch men come in, nothing but smiles and 'What about ya, love?' — and later leave, cursing under their breath. They'd scrunch their betting dockets in their fists and toss them on the floor.

One punter, a once famous snooker player, who spoke in a raspy whisper — he smoked up to eighty cigarettes a day — was always trying to place bets after the off. Sometimes we took them, but if the race was half over, we'd refuse, and he'd call us all the 'bastarding fuckers' of the day. Each evening, while the shop manager counted the day's takings, I'd sweep the floor, brushing scores of crumpled dockets into the dustpan and dumping them in the bin.

I never questioned what my grandfather did for a living. There weren't a whole lot of options available to Catholics when he was starting out (historically, Protestants dominated vital sectors of the Northern Irish economy, like shipbuilding) and he was a good employer. As I got older, I found it more difficult to reconcile the man with the job. Lives were ruined on that shop floor. We were witness to that. We facilitated it.

'Nobody's perfect, Alix,' Mummy said when I asked her about it. 'Your grandfather's a good man. Sure look at Bill Clinton. Can't keep his trousers up, brought peace to Northern Ireland.'

I wasn't sure it was the same thing, but it was good enough for me.

When I was eight years old, Mummy and I were in town on a furious hunt for a pumpkin. My mother loved Halloween. She went to New York one year and was blown away by the costumes and the trick-or-treating and the pumpkin pie. No one celebrated Halloween in Belfast then. You did the dead lists on All Saints' Day. (For the month of November, the church remembers everyone who's died in the previous twelve months. Mummy would drive us around all the churches Mummy Devlin had been associated with when she was alive to drop off the names of our dearly departed. It took us all morning.) But the closest you'd get to an acknowledgement of Halloween was a carved turnip on a windowsill.

Determined to raise the bar, Mummy had received

a tip-off about a gourd delivery at Sawers, a specialist deli on College Street. We were en route when we bumped into a friend of Gogi's. Mum's nostrils immediately began to flare like they always did when she was forced to engage with someone she couldn't stand. She said we couldn't talk – pumpkin-related emergency – and he told her where we could find one. Begrudgingly, she thanked him, and as we turned to go he said, with a smile I didn't quite understand, 'How's your uncle Jimmy doing?'

I was confused. Mummy didn't have an uncle Jimmy. My grandfather was called Jimmy. Maybe that's who he meant.

Mummy tensed, her nostrils dilating to the size of manholes. 'My dad is great, thanks.'

She grabbed me by the hand and walked off. I thought it was an overreaction to an obvious mistake and thought no more of it.

In the early nineties, Daddy Devlin took a back seat in the business while Gogi ran the company with John as his second-in-command. That's when they bought the Malone Road house with its tennis court and en suites. It had five toilets. Five! Had my granny still been alive, she would have chastised her menfolk for their notions. (Irish mothers are obsessed with getting above your station. Everything from espressos to excessive use of toilet roll is 'notion-y'.) It was the privacy the property offered that sold it to my grandfather when Gogi showed him around. There were plenty of secluded spaces where he could read and shut out the outside world.

Wealth didn't change the man. He had exactly three flannel shirts, which he wore on rotation, and on weekends, when Mummy left him and my uncles to fend for themselves, he'd prepare a modest dinner of mackerel and tomatoes to eat in his room. Mummy's other brother and sisters had long moved out, but Gogi and John still lived with their father. Oddly, this had no effect on their pulling power. Each man had their own quarters, where they could entertain overnight guests, of which there were many in Gogi's case. My uncle was handsome, a man of expensive clothes and a full, luxurious moustache. Daddy had a moustache too (Mummy said he needed one because he has a weak upper lip), though it would change on a whim. In the mid-nineties, he experimented with a goatee and when he and Mummy were doing the *Good Life* thing with the goats and the chickens, he went full Brad Pitt in *Legends of the Fall*. Gogi's moustache was more of a Tom Selleck, his chevron a constant throughout the decades, the facial hair of a man comfortable in his skin.

John and Gogi shared the same dark features, a thoroughness of chew ('Nobody can masticate like your grandfather and uncles,' Mummy used to say, alternating between pride and frustration) and a contempt for small talk. Mealtimes were conducted in silence, the moratorium on conversation broken only to talk shop, in sentences composed almost entirely of expletives. This drove my mother mad. 'Stop fuckin' swearin' in front of the girls!' But my sister and I loved our uncles and their awkward ways, especially Gogi. He'd take us out in his red Porsche to the Welcome, the sort of Chinese that offered exoticisms such as water chestnuts and chopsticks. Mummy and Daddy's idea of eastern cuisine was a half roast spring chicken and chips, and curried fried rice.

Occasionally, we'd have company, some groomed glamazon who bought her pants on the Lisburn Road – a popular brunch and boutique spot running parallel with the Malone Road – instead of BHS. They always smelt amazing (the glamazons, not the pants). I used to sneak into my uncle's bathroom after school, before he got home from work, and steal a spritz of the perfume on the windowsill. The scent changed as its wearers came and went. Sometimes, it was joined by an errant face cream, though never for long.

It was a shame. We liked most of Gogi's girlfriends. They made my sister and me feel like we were the women in his life. I guess we were. One of them gave Mummy a mink coat. She said that as it was a hand-me-down and she didn't kill the mink herself, PETA could feck off.

It wasn't always water chestnuts and politically incorrect outerwear. There were bad days too. Like the time Mummy got a phone call from Gogi's golf club and jumped straight into the car, leaving us with Daddy Devlin, who was hanging from a metal bar across the doorway of his bedroom to decompress his spine. An hour later, she arrived home. Daddy and John were behind her, carrying Gogi, his arms draped over their shoulders. He spotted me in the doorway: 'Hey kiddo.' The next day after school, I found him slumped in front of the TV, wearing a pair of grey jogging bottoms and picking at the burnt pork chop Mummy had made him for tea. He was in the jogging bottoms again the day after that. And after that. I thought he'd never get better.

But he did. Mummy took him to a meeting, where they bumped into someone he knew. 'I'm here with my sister. She's the one with the problem,' he told them.

Mummy went along with it. She'd have done anything for her big brother. Before long, he was himself again – my clean-cut, chain-smoking uncle, another perfume bottle on the windowsill. We went back to the Welcome and had our usual order, only Gogi knocked back Perrier instead of vodka tonics. It was years before I saw the tracksuit bottoms again.

4

Give us this day our daily bap

Whenever life gets overwhelming, I crave boiled chicken. Not roast chicken or pan-seared breasts in a herb jus. Just a plain old boiling fowl. There are few things in this world as comforting. Every Saturday, Mummy would baptise a bird in a cauldron of salted water, chucking in a packet of soup mix and chopped veg, then scraping the carcass clean for sandwiches. The bread was sliced white pan or crusty Belfast bap* – none of your fancy stuff, thank you very much.

With the exception of her soup, the woman's culinary skills left a lot to be desired. When uninspired by the contents of her fridge (a frequent occurrence), she'd fry everything in sight – turnip, cabbage, potatoes – in

---

* Crusty on the outside, with a butter-soft interior, the Belfast bap is so beloved, its creator, nineteenth-century baker Barney Hughes, was posthumously awarded a blue plaque near his former home in the city centre. Contrary to the popular children's rhyme, *Barney Hughes's bread, it sticks to yer belly like lead, it ain't a bit of wonder you fart like thunder, Barney Hughes's bread*, the roll is not known to cause excessive flatulence.

an ocean of butter and serve with a couple of fish fingers or a packet of Pasta 'n' Sauce. She referred to this unholy union of leftovers and 'buck-whatever-ya-have-into-the-pot' as a 'skaki', which she liked to smother in brown sauce. She liked to smother everything in brown sauce, from sardines to spaghetti. Daddy was deeply offended by his wife's left-field palate and would look on in horror as she applied all manner of inappropriate condiments to her plate. The greater his disgust, the more outrageous the combinations became. She once ate an entire tin of tuna covered in pepper sauce just to wind him up.

'That'll learn him for being so judgemental,' she said, a shade greener, but jubilant.

Like Mummy says, my father was no Marco Pierre White when they met (although he had the same unkempt head of curls as the restaurant world's *enfant terrible*). Daddy was in his twenties when he had his first mushroom, tinned peas the only vegetable allowed through the front door in his house. My mother, on the other hand, frequently sought out rare foodstuffs at Sawers or from farther afield – twice a year, she imported huge drums of honey from Budapest for my grandfather. (Daddy Devlin had read somewhere that Hungarian bees produce the best acacia.)

Mummy had a natural remedy for every ailment, stewed prunes on a daily basis to keep us regular, and banned us from having a microwave because they 'fry your ovaries'. Perversely, recognising her limitations as a cook or perhaps because she had five siblings, two children, a parent and a husband to feed, she relied heavily on convenience food. On Sundays, the one day of the week she granted us a hiatus from her no-sugar rule, we got stuck into the classics – Heinz treacle sponge pudding in a can or Ambrosia creamed rice with a dollop of gelato from Fusco's ice cream parlour.

This stretch of road, from Sawers up the Falls to Fusco's, was our world. A five-minute walk from the Manse was Daddy's childhood home, where my grand-parents still lived with Daddy's sister Teresa and his aunt Roseleen. We'd visit every Sunday after mass in St Agnes's, the aroma of incinerated silverside – just the way Papa, my paternal grandfather, liked it – greeting us on arrival. Papa wore clear, thick-rimmed glasses and a wide smile. Unlike Daddy Devlin, he *was* the sit-on-my-knee-and-tell-me-about-your-day sort of grandfather, a gentle man of simple tastes. He asked for nothing but frying steak on a Tuesday and an easy life.

Toni and I loved sneaking bites of Teresa's Baileys cheesecake when Mummy wasn't looking. It was a rare treat. Roseleen liked to hide the Baileys bottles in the garage lest they lead Teresa into temptation. Our great-aunt disapproved of many things, especially Dubliners ('tight as anything') and people of colour. (She blessed herself when she heard Uncle John had started seeing a South African. Liz is Afrikaans, but to scandalise the older woman, Mummy told Roseleen she was one of the Swazi tribeswomen, who dance for their men bare-breasted.) Most offensive of all were the police, the devil's foot soldiers. Before the Troubles, the RUC was responsible for the census. An officer called round, leaning a foot on the threshold while Grandma went to find the paperwork. He was barely out the gate when Roseleen had the holy water out, spraying the front door as though she were putting out the Great Fire of London. Her Achilles heel was Mills & Boon. She couldn't get enough of heaving bosoms and lusty farmhands, and prayed to God to release her from her addiction. Once liberated, she saw it as her duty to monitor everyone else's pleasures.

It was your typical Catholic household, the holy water font beside the front door, a St Brigid's Cross tucked behind a picture of Our Lady in the hallway. My Grandma Mary★ said the rosary every evening until the day she died. During the Troubles, she'd tell Papa she was off to pray for peace in a neighbour's garage, carrying a cup of tea and packet of Jammie Dodgers out the door with her rosary beads. Mercifully, Daddy never foisted this involved ritual on our family. He said his prayers each night and took us to mass until we were old enough to go by ourselves. He liked having a couple of pints on a Saturday without enduring the tuts of older worshippers the next day over his less-than-fresh appearance. To assuage the guilt of his no-show, he'd quiz Toni and me after mass on who wrote the Gospel or what the priest said in his sermon. We were always a step ahead, picking up a pamphlet before the service then heading to Fusco's for a banana

---

★ Not to be confused with Mummy Devlin, who was also Mary, which is my middle name and my sister's middle name, and my husband's friend Reginald's middle name. Like I said, we Catholics are big into Our Lady.

split. It was impossible to get a heads-up on the topic of the weekly homily, but Daddy always seemed satisfied with: 'He talked about loving thy neighbour and staying away from all the bad things.'

Mummy didn't care whether we went to mass or not. She was all or nothing in her faith. Months would go by without her uttering so much as a Hail Mary, then suddenly she'd take a notion for confession and jump in the car. When John Paul II died in 2005, she announced she was going to his funeral and asked if I wanted to come along. I was at university in Dublin at the time, and though it wasn't the coolest move to fly a thousand miles to pay your respects to a man who stood for everything students are meant to loathe, I fancied a free trip to Rome. Besides, I had a soft spot for that particular pope. Lots of Irish Catholics did, even us lapsed ones. We joined the other pilgrims in prayer in St Peter's Square, then made our way to a bar around the corner to sink carafes of Gavi in the sun.

Most years, Mummy dragged us along to the novena, nine successive days of mass each June at Clonard, a monastery situated in an interface area between the Falls and the Shankill. The novena became popular during the Troubles, the faithful spilling out into the grounds of the church as loudspeakers mounted to lampposts festooned with bunting in the papal colours of white and yellow played 'Ave Maria'. On the streets surrounding the monastery, vendors hawked sacred heart statues and votives, and there was a Portakabin in the car park where priests doled out penance to those who couldn't squeeze their way through the crowds to the confessional boxes inside. On sunny days, the congregation sat on fold-up chairs in the rose garden, children lying on the grass playing with their trolls and Tamagotchis, while their mothers bowed their heads and prayed for blessings. It was like Glastonbury for Catholics.

Protestants showed up too. For its ecumenical mass, Clonard would invite speakers from different churches to address the faithful. You still get thousands at the novena. They come from all over Belfast and beyond for one of ten daily services – Father Joe was fierce excited when the monastery went live on the 'world wide web' for the first time, allowing those who lived abroad or were unable to make it in person to participate. I told Mummy I'd do a virtual novena with her after I'd left home. I logged on to the Clonard website and there she was with my sister, in a row of seats behind the altar, holding up an A4 piece of paper that read, HELLO OUR ALIX!

When I was preparing for my holy communion aged seven and receiving the obligatory instruction at school on how to be a godly sort, I asked Mummy why Daddy Devlin didn't go to mass. Didn't that make him a bad person? 'There are people who eat the altar rails every Sunday and don't have a Christian bone in their body,' she told me. Mummy did the novena each year, not out of a sense of Catholic duty, but because she liked the singalong the priests did on the final day and was moved by the service that featured the anointing of the sick. She was uplifted and humbled by the petitions and thanksgivings to Our Lady, which the priest would read out after his homily. Scribbled on pieces on paper by members of the congregation and popped into a wooden box at the back of the chapel, prayers ranged from 'Dear Mother of Perpetual Help, can you make sure Celtic win the title next season?' to appreciation for the staff working in the intensive care unit at the Royal Children's Hospital: 'They took such good care of my baby before your son decided it was time for her to go up to heaven.'

The years she wasn't feeling it, when it was too hard to muster gratitude, she didn't go. Irish Catholics are often criticised for their à la carte approach to religion. Apart from Christmas and occasionally Easter, I rarely attend mass, but I can never pass a beautiful chapel without popping in to light a candle for a special intention. I'm not sure where I stand on my faith. I think I believe in God, but I'm pro-choice, spent years on the pill and am angry as hell over the child abuse scandals. Yet I still got married in a Catholic church, christened my babies in one.

It comes down to identity, I suppose. Traditionally, Ireland is a Catholic country and, by and large, Catholics living in Northern Ireland identify as Irish. Religion has become an essential part of who we are, even if we don't subscribe to all its tenets. One of my best friends had a secular wedding (you'd be surprised how rare that is in Ireland, even now). She didn't care about atmosphere or pleasing her parents – the excuses we lapsed Catholics like to peddle to justify our hypocrisy. To her, getting married in a church would be giving tacit approval to everything she abhorred. I can't argue with that point of view, with those who say, 'It's all or nothing, folks – you're either a committed Catholic or nothing at all. Take your pick.' Mummy doesn't share this internal conflict. She says she can disagree with the church and take what she needs from it, and doesn't need to justify herself to anyone.

God, grandparents, ice cream – we had it all in Andytown. There was no need to leave unless you were going on holiday. Occasionally, when we were feeling adventurous, we ventured east – east Belfast, that is. Our dentist, a friend of Gogi's, was based next door to the Ulster Unionist Party headquarters on the Belmont Road, a smart suburb inhabited by well-off Protestants. A few doors down was a shop selling bibles and other Christian paraphernalia, sandwiched between two tea rooms – middle-class Protestants love a traybake. Mummy also took us to less prosperous parts. The residents of the Cregagh Road were more demonstrative in their appreciation for the union, the red, white and blue of the UK's national flag serving as a reminder to outsiders of where allegiances lay. That didn't deter my mother. She took her Halloween parties seriously and Aunt Sandra's Candy Factory did the best toffee apples in town.

There were other benefits to living on the Falls. The area was patrolled by the IRA, who doled out knee-cappings as punishment to local youths who crossed the line. (To be clear, we weren't into vigilantism, though my father found the RUC's response to the theft of his third lawnmower somewhat lacking. When the burglaries suddenly stopped, he half wondered if the 'RA had got wind of his predicament and had had a friendly word with the would-be horticulturist.) Due to our unique judicial system, official bods tended to steer clear. Which is why virtually no one living on the Falls and its environs had a TV licence – the inspectors were too afraid to enter the area to enforce it. It was only when Daddy, who at this stage had his own production company, was about to submit a tender for a commercial aimed at clamping down on TV licence fraud, that he decided the optics weren't great and signed us up for one.

5

The mad woman of Andytown

My mother could be strangely sentimental. The Manse, where she lived from the age of sixteen, and our home when we left the Glen Road, had a huge attic, packed with photo albums and trunks of clothes belonging to Mummy Devlin. Over the years, Mummy added boxes of mementoes from our childhood to the clutter, including the stitches used to piece back together my sister's cheek after she fell through a roof when she was seven.

We were trying to catch a glimpse of the swimming pool in the garden next door to Daddy Devlin's house by clambering on top of our grandfather's log shed. My great idea. Its roof was covered with alternating corrugated iron and acrylic panels, and our Toni stepped on the latter, plummeting straight through and tearing her cheek open. I ran to the house to get Mummy, who wrapped Toni in a blanket and bundled us into the car, the whole time shouting invocations to God, Our Lady, 'Sweet be to fuck Jesus', whoever he was.

A disembodied voice came from the other side of the hedge. 'In our lord's name, is there anything I can do to help?'

Mummy thanked the voice, then sped off to A&E.

Toni was fine. She still has a scar that turns purple when it's cold, reminding me of my failings as an older sibling.

In the middle of the room was a large snooker table we rarely used; in fact, we rarely used the attic at all. Daddy did it up in the style of a gentleman's club after we moved in, in the hope that he and Mummy might entertain friends at the top of the house, but even when the red velvet curtains and embossed wallpaper had been removed, the space remained defiantly Mummy Devlin's.

A small garden filled with blue and white hydrangeas and a rose bush that Mummy Devlin had planted when she moved in, my mother's pride and joy, ran along the side of the house. The back was a less formal arrange-ment – a large rectangle of lawn surrounded by shrubbery. For a while, we'd a homeless man named Podge living in one of the hedges. On the nights he couldn't get into the local shelter, he'd arrive with his sleeping bag, waving through the living-room window as he passed. Podge was a cracking raconteur. Mummy would bring him out clothes and food, and he'd tell us stories about his time in the 'RA during the 'hairy days of the war'. Often, his tales didn't add up. I asked Mummy if she thought Podge had really been in the IRA. She said it didn't matter whether he was or not and to go along with it, that being kind is more important than the truth. 'But what if the truth *is* the kindest thing?' I asked her. She didn't answer.

Toni and I spent a lot of time in the back garden, wheeling and dealing. The oak trees were ripe with fat chestnuts and we capitalised on this bounty, selling them to local lads for up to 50p a piece from my Early Learning Centre market stall. Despite her discomfort at my shameless attempts at profiteering from Andersonstown's conker shortage, my sister went along with it, as she did most of my schemes. There's just two and a half years between us, but Toni would defer to me on all matters, saying nothing the time Moira's daughter Saoirse and I dressed her up as a sumo wrestler and tied her to a lamppost as a social experiment. (An experiment in what, I'm not sure.) Eventually, she realised I didn't have all the answers, and these days has no qualms putting me in my place, but her loyalty has never wavered.

It wasn't long before the locals started to resent this exploitation and decided they'd rather spend their pocket money on Taz bars instead of conkers. They began sneaking into the garden to throw sticks at the trees to relieve them of their treasure. When we caught them in the act, one of them flashed at us. We told Mummy, and the next time they came around she chased them down the street with the hurling stick my dad kept beside their bed (everyone in Andytown kept a hurl beside their bed). Grabbing one by the collar, she said if he touched her trees or exposed his penis to her girls again, she'd lob it off. They called her 'The Mad Woman of Andytown'.

If her reputation as an oddball bothered Mummy, she never let on. In fact, she seemed to welcome the disapproval of others. My mother believed firmly in three things: not turning up to someone's house with your two arms the one length (one arm should be weighed down by a gift for the host), breastfeeding your children off to school, and the daily airing of one's genitalia. She attributes my recurring yeast infections to my refusal to strip off. 'I did not raise my daughters to wear pants in bed,' she admonished me, when a few years back I confessed to keeping my underwear on beneath my pyjamas in winter.

Her naturist leanings weren't exactly orthodox in 1980s Belfast, and I've often asked myself how much this played a part in her implacable belief system, this going against the grain. When Auntie Roseleen said it was cruel to deprive us of chocolate at Easter, Mummy spent all day making eggs out of carob. We arrived at Grandma and Papa's house on Easter Sunday, in matching Laura Ashley dresses (I was twelve), carrying elaborate baskets decorated with handknitted bunnies and chicks.

'Look, Roseleen!' Mummy gestured at her handi-work. 'Delicious *and* good for your teeth. Isn't that right, girls?'

Toni bit an ear off a carob bunny and spat it out.

My mother didn't do girlfriends. She had plenty of them when she was at school, but with the excep-tion of Moira, she let her friendships fall by the wayside over the years. Head of Drama at St Mary's, Daddy's alma mater, Moira coached her students with the zeal of a Premier League football manager, and it showed — her annual musicals were sell-out affairs and many of Moira's boys went on to glittering careers on the London and Dublin stages. Her other passion was Ireland and the promise of its reunification. Linguistics mattered to Moira. It was always 'the north of Ireland', never 'Northern Ireland', a coded identifier that told her all she needed to know about who she was talking to.

Moira was there for all the big events. After my parents' wedding, she flew to London to see them off on the final leg of their honeymoon to Barbados. I think she wanted to make sure Mummy got on the plane. It was the first time she'd left her family to fend for themselves since Mummy Devlin died, and the days leading up to the wedding were a flurry of bread-baking and stocking up on toilet roll. Moira called round to pack Mummy's suitcase with sundresses and jackets she'd worn on her own honeymoon, my mother watching on in disapproval.

'I've already got something for the beach, Moira,' she said, gesturing at a sexless navy one-piece on the bed and removing a pair of high-legged white bikini bottoms from the pile.

Moira snatched the bottoms off her and refolded them, taking a drag of her cigarette with two perfectly manicured scarlet nails. 'Don't give me any shit, girl. You're taking both bikinis. And for fuck's sake, buy yourself a razor, would you? It's like the Black Forest down there.'

My mother wore the bikinis. And the sundresses and the jackets. I see her looking at the photo album of her honeymoon sometimes, her finger tracing the tanned and smiling woman in a white kaftan (ignoring the mullet-ed man on the sand beside her in the world's smallest Speedo).

Whenever Moira visited, Toni and I were expected to hang out with Saoirse. We explained to Mummy that Saoirse would perch on top of the Wendy house in our playroom and demand we 'beat the living crap out of each other' for her delectation, just as we explained to her that the son of one of my father's colleagues decapitated my favourite My Little Pony with his bare hands that time we all went on holiday together to Spain. Our mother didn't want to hear it. (Years later, I worked with a guy who was big into child-led parenting. He told me he and his wife drifted from friends who didn't share their views on raising humans, and wouldn't dream of pushing their children into a friendship merely for their own convenience. My parents and their generational cohort were not of this school of thought. If a friend popped round for a cuppa, nothing short of a stab wound would persuade them to intervene in the enforced bonding of their children. Toni and Saoirse are now best friends, Toni godmother to Saoirse's daughter. For Mummy, this unexpectedly happy outcome has vindicated her theory that most parenting philosophies are a 'load of dick'.

There were other friends in my mother's life at various stages, bodies that filled rooms, sinking pints of Guinness and tapping their feet to the trad bands that played at my parents' annual St Patrick's Day party; that praised Mummy's pumpkin pie as they huddled together in the back garden to watch Daddy nearly blow a hand off attempting to light a Catherine wheel every Halloween. For my father's fortieth, Mummy threw him a surprise party. Five minutes after he left for work that morning, the marquee arrived. She found a pair of knickers in Podge's hedge the next day and was delighted – drunken intercourse was the sign of a good night. It was another one of my mother's contradictions: she preferred her own company, but no one could throw a party like her. Over the years, the parties became less frequent – eventually, they stopped altogether. I used to feel sorry for these unwitting victims of my mother's culls. They never knew what crime they'd committed, which of Mummy's red lines they had crossed (there was only one really – prying into her business, asking too many questions).

My mother's shunning of conventions such as friendship – and appropriate attire – used to bother me. She'd drop us off to school without changing, standing beside the other mums in her dressing gown as she waved us off on day-trips. She did the same thing to Hil and Bernie. *Couldn't she be like everyone else?* Mummy didn't have time for friends, she'd say. She had everything she needed in my father, sister and me, in Daddy Devlin and her siblings – an unmerry band of misfits that somehow worked. Or I thought they did.

After Gogi, there was Mummy, who was eight years younger than her brother. Uncle Gerry came next. A moustachioed taxi driver, who set fire to post boxes in his wilder years (until the 'RA had a quiet word and disabused him of the notion), Gerry was disinclined to look on the bright side of anything, from politics ('Shower of fuckers running the show'), to how Daddy glazed the Christmas ham ('Honey instead of brown sugar? Fuckin' despert, brother'). But there was nothing he wouldn't do for us. When Mummy expressed a desire to travel across the USSR on the Trans-Siberian Railway, he said he'd procure a gun and go with her for protection: 'Can't trust those communist bastards, Anne.' And when Toni and I were older and started to go out in town, he'd insist on picking us up at the end of the night, with the caveat, 'If ya boke in my cab, you owe me twenty quid.'

My godmother, Auntie Hil, was a few years younger than Gerry. As horrified by her brother's coarse assessment of society as she was by my mother's refusal to adhere to its norms, she was forever chastising Mummy for not wearing a bra and Auntie Bernie for only wearing black ones. You could rely on Hil to get a party started, her infectious cackle announcing her arrival before she entered a room. They had a strange relationship, Mummy and Hil. Close, but fraught. Mummy often said Hil suited no one but herself, which, though not entirely inaccurate, seemed harsh. Hil never forgot a birthday or a graduation, marking every meaningful occasion in her nieces' lives with one of her handmade quilts or trinkets.

She told me once the problem with Mummy was that she spent her life trying to please other people. 'Yer ma was always running around. Making ballerina outfits, bringing the travellers in for tea and sending them away with care packages. Then there were all the bloody old people she went to visit. Everyone likes to joke that I'm selfish. I just know how to say no.'

I admired Hil's chutzpah, her rejection of the role of dutiful daughter. Not that anyone expected her to land the part. Hil was fourteen when Mummy Devlin died. It was always going to be Mummy who filled their mother's shoes. And although I never heard her complain about the cards fate had dealt her, I wondered what she might have done had she taken a leaf out of Hil's book and said no more often. (I don't have to wonder anymore. She told me not long ago she was set to spend three months volunteering in a kibbutz when Mummy Devlin got sick. They were all the rage in the seventies.)

There was just eighteen months between Hil and John, who, after a rocky start when Hil put a broom through the glass panel of the front door trying to whack her younger brother across the head, became thick as thieves. They made a peculiar double act, Hil the life and soul of the party, John grumbling from the sidelines with a whiskey in hand. Bernie, the youngest in the family, was a baby when my parents started going out. Twelve years older than me, she liked the good things in life – red wine and heavy metal. I used to lie on her bed, watching her gel her perm as she blasted Bon Jovi. I wanted to be Bernie when I grew up. Bernie and Kelly Kapowski from *Saved by the Bell*.

I saw my aunts and uncles most days after school. We'd drive over from the Glen Road to the Manse, a pot of stew wedged between my feet in the front seat, the empty pot carried back with us later that evening, its contents replenished the next day and the day after that. For more than a decade, my feet stank of stew and chicken soup and anything else you could fit into an industrial-sized pot. Once, the stew fell on the driveway outside Daddy Devlin's and Mummy scooped it up and threw it back in, gravelly bits and all. When she wasn't making stew, Mummy liked to take part in radio competitions and won that many phone-ins, the station wouldn't let her enter anymore. She started going by various *noms de plume* – Tina Gibson and Anne Plongeur, all for a box of Nambarrie tea bags and a Downtown Radio mug. Knitting was another cherished pastime. She had no interest in the craft until Mummy Devlin, who had tried to teach her daughter on numerous occasions, died, then she asked a friend to teach her. Jumpers, hamburgers (because who doesn't enjoy knitted fast food?) – she can turn her needles to anything. Her greatest triumph was a pair of socks. You're not a real knitter until you can turn the heel of a sock, Mummy Devlin used to say. And whatever my mother undertook, she was determined to be the best at.

After Uncle Gerry and my aunts moved out, Mummy had more time on her hands and was ready for a bigger challenge. When Gogi asked her to attend a meeting of the Belfast and Ulster Licensed Vintners Association, the representative body of bar owners in the city, on his behalf, she went along and by the end of the session had been appointed chairman of the organisation. Before long, she was asked to head up the Federation of the Retail Licensed Trade, which represented some 1,500 publicans across Northern Ireland. She was the first and only woman to hold the post.

Mummy sat Toni and me down at the kitchen table when I was seven and told us things would change if she accepted the role. She wouldn't always be around when we got home from school. There'd be trips abroad. I suspected these absences meant greater opportunities for presents and wished her well in her endeavours. She began travelling throughout Europe and wine-tasting in French chateaux (or pretending to taste wine. She didn't drink at that stage. Daddy says it was a shocking waste). On a visit to a brewery in Hamburg, she addressed her hosts in German. She'd hired a lecturer at Queen's University to translate her speech and practised her delivery every night for a week with Daddy Devlin, who, naturally, had taught himself the language.

Our mother was calmer when she started working. Less likely to roll down the car window and yell 'dick features' to drivers who cut her off. Life was good. She talked about buying herself a sports car and driving through Paris with the warm wind in her hair, like Lucy Jordan in that song sung by Marianne Faithfull. And she did. Years later, she and Daddy cruised along the Champs-Élysées on a warm spring afternoon in an open-top Mazda.

There's a wall in my father's study covered in dozens of photographs of Mummy from her Federation years, her tiny frame in a mayoral-style gold chain, beaming amid a phalanx of greying men in suits. He was proud of her. We all were, though it was strange seeing her in black patent heels and tailoring after a lifetime of tracksuits. She even started wearing a bra.

6

The ugly game

'I don't know, Anne. I swore I'd never set foot in the place again. What's that? I can't hear you with this racket. Hang on a sec.'

My father reaches over the fax machine on the desk in his office and bangs on the radio as the Fresh Prince is about to embark on his fourth *Well yo are y'all ready for me yet?* 'That's the last time I listen to Cool FM. Pile of shite what passes for music these days. So, you've tickets to tonight's game, then?'

Mummy has been invited as a guest of Guinness to watch Northern Ireland play the Republic in the World Cup qualifier at Windsor Park and is trying to convince my dad to go with her. It's set to be a tense fixture. Jackie Charlton's boys are just one step away from getting through to USA '94. Already eliminated, Northern Ireland have no interest in giving their rivals an easy ride. 'It's our intention to stuff the Republic,' said NI's manager Billy Bingham ahead of the game, riled by ROI fans chanting 'There's only one team in Ireland', when the teams met in Dublin in March.

Until last week, it was touch and go whether the match would go ahead. Tensions have been running high in Belfast after Paddy McMahon, a twenty-three-year-old Catholic, was shot dead by the UDA, the first of twenty-six deaths in Northern Ireland in less than three weeks. The violence included the 'trick or treat' massacre – members of the Ulster Freedom Fighters burst into the Rising Sun pub in Greysteel, County Derry, during a Halloween party, one shouting 'Trick or treat' as they opened fire on revellers. The bar had been targeted because it was popular with Catholics who lived in the area.

Security forces and the Irish football associations decided against moving to a neutral venue, but have advised the ROI team to fly to Belfast instead of travelling by road. My father's objections to going to Windsor Park are more personal. He had been a regular spectator at Linfield FC's home ground in south Belfast in the 1960s, back when George Best played for Northern Ireland. During a match between Linfield and east Belfast team Glentoran, Linfield supporters began singing 'God Save the Queen'. The Glentoran crowd retaliated with 'The Sash', a loyalist song commemorating King William III's victory in the Williamite War in the late seventeenth century. 'It was like they were trying to out-Protestant each other,' Daddy said.

It's always been this way. Everything is politics in Northern Ireland, especially football. Catholics support

Celtic; Protestants, Rangers. My lot get behind the Republic of Ireland, whereas Northern Ireland is regarded as a Prod team. It's been said Everton fans in the region tend to be Catholics and that Liverpool appeals to the other side. It wouldn't surprise me. Ireland has one rugby team, yet sectarianism in Northern Irish football is rife. Here, it's not just a bunch of lads kicking a ball around a pitch. It's an expression of identity – and the divide.

Daddy had been planning on watching the match at home with a few tins of Harp, he tells my mother.

'Go on, Micky. It'll be a treat,' she says. 'We'll probably be in a big corporate box and I'm sure they'll put on a huge spread.' Thanks to Mummy's role in the Federation, my parents have become regular guests of Guinness at various events and are always taken care of.

'Aye, it does sound tempting. Alright, I'm in. I'm sure there'll be no issues this time.'

The Guinness depot backs onto the Windsor Park stadium. As Mummy predicted, the drinks giant pulls out all the stops. Guests are treated to a sit-down meal and free-flowing alcohol in a swanky marquee. When it's time to go next door for the match, there's no box, only three rows of reserved seats in the stalls. My parents are split up, Mummy seated next to a representative of Guinness Ireland and other VIPs, while Daddy is five seats away to her right.

The crowd erupts as the teams are led onto the pitch by the referee, and burst into Glasgow loyalist song 'We Are the Billy Boys'. A favourite among Rangers fans, it was banned from Scottish football for its sectarian lyrics. The Northern Ireland manager appears and waves his arms up and down in the air in encouragement. My dad swallows the rising panic in his throat. *It's the man's last game before he retires*, he tells himself. *They're just showing their support.*

And then, a voice in his ear, gravelly, dripping with venom. 'And we're up to our knees in Fenian blood.'

The most controversial line in the song. My father jumps and looks behind him. A man in his fifties, wearing a brown leather jacket and a snarl, is staring straight at him. Dad's stomach lurches. *How does he know I'm Catholic?*

It's time for the national anthems. Only 'God Save the Queen' is played. The Irish Football Association ruled against the Republic's anthem '*Amhrán na bhFiann*' – too provocative. There's only a handful of Republic fans in the crowd anyway, the heightened tension leading up to the match forcing many to abandon their plans to travel north. The game kicks off and my mother, oblivious to Daddy's interaction with the man behind him, is getting into it, clapping and whooping in support of both teams. Northern Ireland score and the crowd goes wild. She cheers with them.

It happens in a flash. A man with a shaved head, two rows in front of my dad, jumps over the back of the seats and pushes his way through the spectators until his face is inches away from my mother's.

He points an accusatory finger at her. 'Fuck you. Fuck you, you Fenian whore.'

Mummy freezes as the man continues his tirade.

Play it cool, Micky. Don't react. You can't afford to get angry.
My father catches Mummy's eye and mouths, 'Do you want to leave?' She nods, the colour drained from her face, and he makes his way over to her past the Guinness rep and the other VIPs, who say nothing, fix their gaze straight ahead. My parents reach the steps as the fans beside them pick up a chant from the other side of the pitch. It's hard to discern at first, but it's clear as anything now: 'Trick or treat, trick or treat.'

They head down the steps – not too quickly; they don't want to draw any more attention to themselves – and pass underneath the stands. Above, someone shouts, 'Your mother is a pope-sucking whore' at one of the ROI players. (Six of Charlton's team, plus the two subs, were born in England, their only connection to the Republic through a grandparent. It's likely their mothers are English Protestants.)

As they reach the car park, others start to trickle out, taking hurried steps towards the exit. One man, shaking his head in disbelief, turns to my mother: 'My son is an excellent footballer, but over my dead body he'll play for them.'

Daddy pushes on the gate. It rattles against a thick padlock. Someone runs to find a member of staff to let them out. More people filter out from the stalls, glancing behind them as they leave. Mummy's shivering now and Daddy pulls her close to him. Eventually, a guard arrives and they're out, the air less toxic beyond the stadium's walls. They hear a muted cheer as they rush to the car. The Republic of Ireland have equalised. They're going to the World Cup.

A week later, the head of Guinness Northern Ireland sends Mummy a huge bunch of lilies and roses, and a letter of apology. He wasn't at the match and tells my mother he's shocked and embarrassed by what happened. The following year, the company flies Mummy out to New York to watch Ireland take on Italy in the World Cup. She has a blast. But it takes my father a little longer to forgive those who sat and watched as they were driven from the stadium.

The night goes down as one of the most tense moments in Irish football history. ROI player Niall Quinn recalls driving to the stadium through the streets of Belfast with his teammates, the lights of their bus turned off, armed escorts in front and behind them, an armed guard on the bus.

'I remember seeing a group of young kids with sticks pretending they were rifles and they were pointing them at us. They'd shoot, kneel down and another row would shoot. I thought: *Jesus, this is crazy stuff.*'

'Would you ever go back to Windsor Park?' I ask my father long after the Troubles had ended.

Sworn enemies Ian Paisley and Martin McGuinness are now sitting side by side in Stormont. Times have changed, wounds have healed, haven't they?

'Never,' he says. 'It still hurts too much, love.'

7

Michael Flatley's magic legs

If you're into papier-mâché, then Anthea Turner's Tracy Island was a masterpiece. Word is, around a hundred thousand children requested the factsheet on how to make the *Thunderbirds* model HQ after tuning in to see Turner's 'Here's one I made earlier'. Personally, I didn't understand what the fuss was about. I enjoyed arts and crafts as much as the next child, but I never really got *Blue Peter*. All those preternaturally cheery presenters with their Benetton jumpers and their tortoises – it was too wholesome (this was pre Richard Bacon's cocaine scandal and Anthea's affair and John Leslie's . . . whatever that was) – and so very *English*.

There was no shortage of excellent kids' TV in the nineties. *Going Live*'s Trev and Simon were small-screen gold. Every Saturday morning, Toni, Daddy and I would join the duo and swing our pants over sausages and potato bread. But I didn't hear anyone who sounded like me, didn't see my experience reflected in the programmes we watched or the books we read. Even for those in Northern Ireland who identified as British, it was hard to relate to the Anglo-centric mindset that dominated the UK's cultural scene. Britishness and Englishness were one and the same.

Not that TV across the border was more inclusive, mind. (Or enjoyable – anyone who found the puppet extra-terrestrials Zig and Zag entertaining needed their head checked.) The Prods thought we Catholics watched RTÉ all the time, but really it only appealed to grannies, who were mad into *Glenroe*, and *The Angelus*, a minute-long moment of reflection broadcast every day before the six o'clock news. As the bells of St Mary's Pro-Cathedral in Dublin chimed, good, godly folk across the country would down tools – the dairy farmer loosening his grip on an udder to bow his head in reverence to Our Lady, the stay-at-home mum abandoning the spud-peeling to have an old pray. Detractors have questioned the relevance of the seventy-year-old tradition in recent years, but *The Angelus* rings on. Its enduring popularity has less to do with devoutness now. It's become part of the Republic's cultural heritage, as Irish as funerals website rip.ie, and breakfast rolls.

American kids' shows were infinitely superior. Toni and I couldn't get enough of Alex Mack and Captain Planet, who, incidentally, embarked on a brief hiatus from 'taking pollution down to zero' to stop Northern Ireland's lawless Catholics and Protestants from wiping each other out in a nuclear holocaust. The episode, 'If it's doomsday, it must be Belfast', was banned by the Northern Irish government. For some reason, the powers that be felt cartoon characters chucking Molotov cocktails at their neighbours didn't quite have that reach-for-the-sky message we've come to expect from children's animation.

Still, my fascination with all things American was unshakeable. I was determined to move to New York the minute I turned eighteen and become an FBI agent. A call to one of Gogi's friends, who worked in the US embassy in Dublin, firmly knocked this ambition on the head. You need to be an American citizen to be in the FBI. She also kindly informed me that the bureau's training academy was in Virginia, not New York, which somewhat dulled the glamour of the job. What was it about America I loved? Kids across the pond had adventures – the Goonies searching for One-Eyed Willie's treasure, Kevin McCallister protecting his home from the bad guys . . . They weren't sitting around fiddling with sticky-back plastic. Plus, the Americans seemed to have a soft spot for Northern Ireland. To our neighbours on the 'mainland' and across the border, we were a bunch of savages with bad moustaches and an axe to grind. But to the Americans, we were misunderstood. They didn't see us as this tiny, irrelevant corner of the UK. We had an ally. (I was eleven at the time, so clearly, none of this really registered. Mainly, I wanted to live in the US because Jonathan Taylor Thomas from *Home Improvement* lived there, and he was a ride.)

This mutual love-in proved lucrative. Once a year, Gogi hosted a party for his American friends, wealthy New Yorkers with names like Joe O'Reilly and Seamus O'Callaghan, who'd come to town for a charity golf tournament. (Rich Americans were always hosting benefits to help The Cause, which essentially equated to filling the coffers of the 'RA.) Toni and I got to go along with Saoirse, as Mummy would organise the whole shindig – tables of cold meats and salads, Irish stew and wheaten bread, giant meringues and Black Forest gateaux, and keg upon keg of Guinness. She'd hire a trad band, and the Americans would arrive in Aran jumpers and Paddy caps and ask the lads if they had any Enya in their repertoire. By the end of the night one of the yanks would get all misty eyed and, clutching their Jameson, ask if we'd indulge them in an Irish jig.

It's a common misconception that all Catholics can Irish dance. Lots of my friends did – I went to school with a girl who ended up touring the world with *Riverdance*. But early on my mother identified that Irish dancing is an involved pastime, requiring a willingness on her part to sacrifice weekends to arrange hair into tightly packed rollers and traverse the country so her daughters could perform at *feiseanna*,* and frankly, Mummy told us, she couldn't have been arsed. Our lack of skill or, indeed, rhythm didn't seem to bother Gogi's friends. One year, one of the guests was so impressed with our 1-2-3s, he fell into a hydrangea bush while engaged in a vigorous round of applause. (He later blamed his lack of balance on 'that third pint o' the black stuff'. That's the thing about Irish Americans – they can't drink for shit.) We went home that night with a rake of fifty-dollar bills.

I was happy to oblige the Americans with this

---

* Irish dance competitions.

performative display of Irishness, but truth be told, I wore my heritage lightly. I didn't play camogie★ or speak Irish – I never managed to get beyond the first line of the Irish national anthem, even the English version. My classmates, among whom were the nieces of Gerry Adams and Bobby Sands (the republican hunger striker, whose death in Long Kesh – Protestants called it The Maze – prison in 1981 led to a surge in IRA recruitment), spent their summers at the *Gaeltacht* in Donegal and a number had family in the IRA. Which was a shock after seven sheltered years in the tiny primary school next door, a place where sectarian meant a really old person.

I remember the exact date I felt Irish, and proud to be Irish, for the first time. It's 30 April 1994. I'm watching Eurovision with my family, as we do every year. Daddy has themed dinner to the cuisine of the country that won the previous year. (Ireland's been on a winning streak, so he hasn't had to stretch himself too much.) We're particularly excited this Eurovision, because Daddy filmed four of the 'postcards', the forty-second clips played before performers take to the stage, showcasing what Ireland has to offer (namely churches and pubs).

We're sitting around the TV, plates of sausages and champ† on our laps and there's this voice, haunting and hypnotic, and then more voices, a chorus of mystical beings in hooded capes. A goddess, in an

---

★ Irish sport, similar to hurling.
† Mashed potato with spring onion.

off-the-shoulder black dress, bounces on stage and her red hair bounces with her, but it looks like her real hair and not a wig, and this is unusual for an Irish dancer. She's gone now . . . but wait – who's this? A man with a mullet and a billowing silk shirt has appeared and he's doing mind-blowing things with his feet and now he's having a dance-off with four *bodhráns* and he knows he's doing unholy things with his feet, because he's pointing at them and smiling a smile that says, 'Yes, I'm half-man, half-god'.

The goddess is back and they're dancing together, and sweet baby Jesus, they make a sexy pair. And Mummy is saying, 'Who is this Michael Flatley? I'd do a turn with him.' And Daddy's not even disgusted, because he looks like he'd like to do a turn with him too. And now there's a load of them dancing, what must be forty pairs of legs moving in unison and the crescendo builds and there's more tapping and then it's over and everyone in the audience is on their feet. And Terry Wogan (because we always watch the BBC coverage of Eurovision and not RTÉ's, then complain that Terry's forgotten his roots and should be presenting the RTÉ coverage of Eurovision and not the BBC's) says, 'Small hairs are rising on the back of every Irishman's neck.'

In that seven-minute interval, everything changed for Ireland. Michael Flatley's magic legs put the country on the map, changing the narrative from poverty, bad food and shite weather to something cooler, more global. Everyone wanted to be Irish, myself included. After Eurovision, I dug out Daddy's U2 CDs in an attempt to connect with my newly discovered identity. Daddy was thrilled I was finally taking an interest in the mother culture and gave me books on Irish history and the Troubles to read. I gathered them in a pile beside my bed, where they remained unread until it was time to box them up when my parents were moving house years later.

8

Bill and the British bastard

My best friend at primary school was a girl called Danielle. She had a face full of freckles, and a sister, Helen, who was in Toni's year. The four of us were inseparable and, along with Saoirse, the founding members of a number of clubs and societies, which I insisted on chairing from our garden shed.

Every Friday night we'd head to Danielle and Helen's, their mother sending us to their local Chinese takeaway for chips to go with her homemade chicken curry. We knew the owners – their daughter Cynthia was in our class at school. She joined in P6 after her family moved to Belfast from Hong Kong. This was a source of great excitement among my classmates, with everyone wanting to befriend the wee Chinese girl. Danielle and I would soon be going to different schools and promised to stay in touch. But when she scooped the role of Mary in the Nativity, swiftly followed by Dorothy to my Tinman in the P7 production of *The Wizard of Oz*, things were never the same and we went our separate ways.

My first day at St Dominic's, Mummy ditched the dressing down and wore proper clothes to drop me off. Times had changed now she was a working woman. We parked the car outside St Paul's church and walked past the corner shop through a throng of maroon pinafores and platform Kickers. A group of older girls stood outside eating Monster Munch and removing gold hoops from straining earlobes and Claddagh rings from greasy fingers. Wiping their hands on their blazers, they pocketed their contraband and made their way through the gate in the stone wall surrounding the school. I had no earrings to hide from the teachers as Mummy said if Mother Nature wanted me to be perforated, She'd have done it herself. (Funnily enough, Mother Nature had less of an issue with Mummy colouring her greys.)

That's where I met Aisling (the classmate who revealed the sorry truth about Santa) for the first time – at the school gates, when our mothers got chatting and pushed us together. Aisling nodded. 'Alright?' And I smiled maniacally and said this was the best day of my life and did she want to see my new pencil case. She narrowed her eyes and we walked in silence along the path leading to the old part of the school, a nineteenth-century red-brick building that housed the convent and assembly hall. The school was founded by the Dominican order, but by the time I started there were only a handful of nuns left on the teaching staff, including Sister Frances, the headmistress. I can't recall anything Sister Frances said in her welcome address that morning. Something about veritas, no doubt. Our teachers drilled our school motto into us daily – that truth is the mother of all virtues – which sort of flew in the face of Mummy's 'Be kind above all things' ethos.

I do remember the smell of polished wood and Charlie Red body spray, and a sense of panic rising in my throat when Aisling spotted friends from her old school after assembly and ran ahead while I waited on our form tutor to show us to class.

A girl wearing three scrunchies – two around a tightly coiled, hair-sprayed bun and one on her wrist – approached. 'Here, wee girl.'

I looked around.

'Yeah, you.'

The girl pulled a stick of Juicy Fruit out of the breast pocket of her blazer and popped it in her mouth. 'What's going on with the kebs?' she said, appraising my Clarks penny loafers.

'Ummm . . .'

'Cut it out, Colleen.' Another girl with porcelain skin appeared beside Scrunchies and shoved her out of the way. 'Don't listen to her. She's nathin but a big millbeg, aren't ya, Colleen?'

'Fuck off, Pauline.' Colleen raised her middle finger at the alabaster-skinned girl. I gasped.

'Don't worry – she's sound really. I'm Pauline, this is Kelly,' Pauline said, slapping the back of a small girl beside her. 'I think we're in the same class – want to walk with us?'

Pauline and Kelly were my saviours that first term and didn't make fun of me when I brought them back to mine for the first time and suggested we play with

Esberg, my troll. (Mummy brought her back from a Federation trip to Denmark along with a boy troll, Carl, for Toni. I can't imagine many kids had dolls named after a global beer giant, but Daddy was proud with his creative input.) I struggled, though, to adjust to my new surroundings. I didn't know lunchboxes (especially those shaped like giant Micky Mouse heads) and Protestants were out, and went from wanting to be the centre of attention to wanting to fall off the face of the earth. Thankfully, I wasn't the only one who didn't have a clue.

'Girls, meet Natalie. Her family has just moved to Belfast all the way from Dublin and I'd like you to give her a big St Dominic's welcome.'

Sister Frances nudges a girl with gold-red hair in front of the blackboard, nods at Mrs Gough and turns on her heel.

'Did you hear that, girls?' says our French teacher. 'A real St Dominics's welcome for Natalie. *Bonjour*, Natalie.'

'Bout ye!' shouts Colleen from the back of the room. The class starts to snigger.

I'm five months into my first year at St Dominic's. Tight alliances have already been formed, but fresh blood is always exciting. At break-time, a crowd forms around the new girl. Aisling demands Nat recite Boyzone lyrics 'in a Dublin accent'. She appears to do a decent job, as Aisling decides she's dead on and can sit with her crowd at lunch.

Colleen isn't won over just yet. 'What if she's a Free Stater?'

'What's a Free Stater?' I ask Pauline.

'They left Norn Iron behind after the War of Independence and don't want a united Ireland. Fuckers.'

Nat doesn't have time to confirm or deny the accusation, as Sheila Magee has a far worse insult up her sleeve. 'She's a British bastard is what she is.'

A collective gasp as the crowd parts. Sheila is leaning against the wall of the gym, stroking her arse-length plait.

Nat's taken aback by the aggression, but quickly regains composure. 'Erm, hardly. I was born in Galway and spent my whole life in Dublin.'

I'm impressed. Nobody stands up to Sheila. Well, Aisling, but that's it. Chastised, Sheila breaks out the rhetorical big guns – 'Yer ma's yer da' – and walks off with a mutinous swish of her braid.

It's hard to speak to Nat over the next few days as she's always with Aisling and her crew. Later that week, we get chatting outside the mobile huts, waiting for biology to start. We discover Nat's dad and Gogi went to school together. Her parents are from Northern Ireland originally, moving to Dublin before Nat was born, and her dad's business has brought them back north. (Another thing we have in common is the weight of deceit on our young shoulders. Like me, Nat only got wise to the Saint Nic. fraud aged ten, when she asked a Protestant she'd just met whether they celebrated Christmas.)

That night, I tell Mummy about the new girl and the family connection. She insists I invite Nat over for a barbecue the following weekend even though it's the middle of February. Mummy does stuff like that – al fresco dining in winter, turf fires in the middle of August. Be damned with the naysayers. I spend all week arranging an afternoon of top entertainment. When Nat arrives, I bring her up to the playroom for some dress-up, then after lunch suggest we take the scooters Toni and I got for Christmas out for a spin before heading to Fusco's for a poke. I think Nat must be a bit special, because she's got a really weird look on her face, then I realise she's unfamiliar with Belfast parlance for an ice cream cone. When Nat's mum arrives to pick her up that evening, I'm sure I've blown it.

On Monday morning, I'm on the floor outside the assembly hall behind Aisling and her gang, blissing out to Enigma's 'Return to Innocence' on my Discman – *Uh-yi-aiiiii uh yi-yi-yi* – when I spot Nat coming up the stairs.

Don't care what people say
Just follow your own way . . .

Heading in our direction, she waves at Aisling as she passes, then flops down beside me, grinning. And that's the day I become best friends with a British bastard.

Nat lived a five-minute drive from Daddy Devlin, Gogi and John. Her house had cream carpets and radiator covers in every room, and in the downstairs toilet, magnolia room spray from M&S and a wooden sign that said, *If you sprinkle when you tinkle, please be sweet and wipe the seat.* I loved going back to Nat's after school.

We'd pop a couple of Bird's Eye waffles in the toaster and watch Trouble TV, Nat's mum checking in on us from time to time, all smiles and immaculate blow-dries. My mother didn't do blow-dries. Her hairdresser Michelle would come round to the house every three weeks to dye her hair, but was never allowed to stay long enough to finish the job. Mummy was always in a rush to get over to my granddad's in time for tea. She'd pay Michelle then pack us into the car, wiping blobs of Clairol Mocha Splash off her forehead as she reversed out of the garage.

Nat shared a room with her older sister Kate. I'd stay over in her bed when Kate visited friends in Dublin. You were always guaranteed a sound night's sleep at Nat's house. Her mum had an electric blanket on every bed and Nat would play a CD of Care Bears bedtime stories to help her drift off. At home, we drifted off to the sound of screeching breaks when the local hoods went on their nightly joyride. Nat's room had a Sliderobe that spanned the length of the back wall and was bursting with mini dresses and spaghetti tops. Toni and I rarely shared clothes. Her Sporty Spice phase lasted until she went to university. Besides, she had no interest in dressing like a mad aunt. (I thought I had a good eye, but on reflection, the patchwork skirt embroidered with tiny bells that rang when you walked, which I wore for our first non-uniform day, was sartorial suicide.)

There was something reassuringly normal about Nat's family. Her mum apologised whenever Nat's dad swore during the horse racing (but given Mummy's family's fondness for imprecations, it would take a lot more than an 'Ah, fuck it' to scandalise me) and to my knowledge, Nat's parents never chased one another around the back garden bollock naked, like mine did after Daddy cut off his ponytail and Mummy decided she fancied him all over again.

We hung out for the rest of the year until June, when Nat went on her annual family holiday to Majorca, then back to Dublin, and Toni and I headed to Connemara for the summer with Mummy and Daddy Devlin. When we reunited for our second year that September I was dismayed to discover I had competition for Nat's attentions. Mel had just transferred from Rathmore, a co-ed Catholic school in south Belfast and one of Northern Ireland's leading grammars, ostensibly because St Dominic's had a better music department and Mel was a gifted pianist. (She also played the clarinet – the talent was sickening.) But Nat told me Mel's brother hurled himself out of a tree on the school grounds, breaking a leg. Sensing a similarly adventurous streak in her daughter, Mel's mother decided a convent school with less inviting tree trunks was the prudent option.

Nat and Mel met on the minibus that took the few south Belfast-based St Dominic's pupils to school. They bonded one morning after the bus was egged by some lads from Corpus Christi, an all-boys secondary school in Beechmount, just off the Falls Road proper. It was a concerning development and I couldn't stop thinking about Nat and Mel watching Trouble TV at Nat's, Mel helping herself to my waffles. If I wanted to keep Nat in my life, I had to befriend Mel.

Granted, there are better ways to go about getting someone to be your friend than stalking them. Mel was in a different class from Nat and me, so I started waiting for her in the corridor outside the music room and would thrust letters into her hand, my blazer covering my face to maintain an air of mystery. The content of the communication varied. Generally, it was along the lines of:

I've kidnapped your friend Paula. If you want to see her again, meet me at Spring Fry after school for a chip butty.

Then there was the Saturday Pauline and I walked the mile-and-a-half journey from the Manse to Cranmore Park beside Mel's house to see where she lived. We hadn't counted on bumping into Mel, who was out walking her dog. 'Er, hi guys.' She sounded freaked out. 'Are you here to see me?'

'No, no, we're just in the area.' *Be cool, Alix.* 'Nat said Barnams does better pokes than Fusco's and I find that hard to believe, so we thought we'd check it out.'

I have to say, Mel handled it well, recommending the knickerbocker glory. She had a piano lesson that afternoon, but next time, we should all go to Barnams together. Privately, she asked Nat if I was all there and Nat assured her I was harmless. That was good enough for Mel, and though she was still more Nat's friend then, I realised she was alright actually, and that there were more than enough waffles to go around.

It took Nat a while to get used to a west Belfast education. On a theatre trip to London not long after they'd moved, her sister Kate found herself comforting a classmate who was upset she wasn't at home for April Fool's Day.

'It's just that we have a tradition – every year, we hide my daddy's prosthetic hand,' said the girl, holding back tears.

'God, what happened to him?' asked Kate.

'Ach, it was blown off making a wee bomb for the 'RA.' (Could this have been the infamous Jim Davey who'd made a pipe bomb without a vice?)

The following year, the bell for home time was about to ring when our year head Mrs Conlon hurried into the room and whispered in Miss Rooney's ear.

The history teacher tutted and looked at her watch, greatly inconvenienced by the news. 'Girls, I'm afraid you'll have to stay where you are,' she said. 'There's been an incident.'

It was an hour before we were allowed out. The next day, we found out there'd been an INLA★ shooting outside the school and the gunmen had tried to escape via the hockey pitch.

'Christ on a bike!' Nat shook her head. Colleen had just finished giving us the lowdown in the queue for the tuck shop. Nat opened her bag of Space Raiders and shared them around. 'You're all fucking mad up here, Lix.'

She got used to the madness eventually. You had no choice. We couldn't let stuff like that bother us. For one thing, we were teenagers. By definition, we were

★ Irish National Liberation Army, a breakaway group of the Official IRA. They are notorious for, among other incidents, the car bomb that killed Conservative MP Airey Neave outside the House of Commons in 1979, the Droppin' Well pub bombing of 1982 and the shooting dead of three UVF members on the Shankill Road in 1994.

solipsistic assholes. There was no room in our undeveloped brains to contemplate life beyond boys, booze and Boyzone. Anyway, violence was part and parcel of living in Northern Ireland. On 23 October 1993, the year before Nat moved to Belfast, two IRA members disguised as delivery men walked into Frizells' fish shop on the Shankill Road, carrying a bomb. It detonated prematurely, killing ten, including Michelle Morrison, aged seven, and Leanne Murray, who was thirteen. The murders resulted in the biggest revenge attacks of the Troubles. Fourteen Catholics were killed the following week.

I don't remember my reaction. Isn't that weird? I don't remember what I thought about something so unthinkable. Perhaps it's because we never talked about stuff like that at home. Whenever there was another bomb or a shooting on the news, Daddy would sigh and go back to reading the *Mirror* and Mummy would say it was 'desperate' and continue to roll sticks of newspaper for the fire. I never thought to say, 'How do you *feel* about this? Isn't it messed up?' There would have been little point. My parents would have agreed that yes, it is messed up, but it's life, get on with it. Because that's what you did.

An off-duty policeman was having a quiet drink with his brother in one of our family's pubs on a Saturday afternoon in 1992 when the IRA shot him dead. Mummy went in early on the Monday morning. She scrubbed the policeman's blood off the vinyl upholstery on the bar stool where he sat so the staff wouldn't have to see it, came home and got us ready for school.

It was never mentioned. Nor did she mention the body parts she saw the time the White Fort pub, two doors down from the Manse, was bombed at the start of the Troubles. Peeling potatoes in the kitchen with Mummy Devlin, she heard the explosion and ran out onto the street with her mother, blankets to cover the wounded under their arms.

Daddy's brother, Uncle Ted, was meant to be meeting friends there that evening, changing his mind about going out at the last minute. A firefighter throughout most of the conflict, Ted once told Daddy about the day he was called out when an incendiary device went off on a train somewhere between Belfast and Lisburn, killing one person. His team couldn't lift the dismembered body in one go, so Ted had to shovel it in parts. It was the first and last time he talked to anyone about his work.

Northern Ireland has the highest rate of mental health illness in the UK, at least 25 per cent higher than England. We have significantly higher rates of depression, self-harm, antidepressant use and the highest rate of suicide of all the regions.

Yet the proportion of spend on mental health remains the lowest in the UK. More people have taken their own lives since the Good Friday Agreement was signed in 1998 than died in the Troubles.* Experts attribute

---

* In 2018, Northern Ireland had a suicide rate of 18.6 per 100,000 people, while England's rate was nearly half that at 10.3 per 100,000 people. Between 2000 and 2018, a total of 4,783 deaths were registered as suicide in Northern Ireland. (Data supplied by the Northern Ireland Statistics and Research Agency, 2018)

the crisis to a perfect storm of drug use, austerity, continued paramilitary violence and intergenerational trauma.

Mental health problems are the legacy of our mess. When my parents were growing up, there was no vocabulary for trauma, no 'safe space' to share. Therapy? Catch yerself on. Anxiety and depression – these were indulgences you didn't entertain. In some ways, that stoicism was passed down to my generation. My friends and I weren't stifled – we felt all the emotions you're meant to feel at that age, and keenly. But we made light of the negative feelings. There was always someone who had it worse. I remember having boy troubles at university around the time foreign nationals were being kidnapped in Iraq and was feeling sorry for myself. Mummy's words of comfort? 'At least you're not that poor Ken Bigley.'

That's not to say we never let our guard down. When the IRA declared a ceasefire in August 1994, everyone was emotional, even Mummy. She picked us up from school and we drove to the Sinn Féin headquarters down the road from the Manse with Auntie Bernie and our cousins. The whole way, horns blasted and tricolours waved out of car windows. I saw big, fat tears rolling down the cheeks of a man with a Celtic cross tattooed on his bicep.

A year later, Bill Clinton came to Northern Ireland, the first sitting US president to visit the region. Mummy wrapped us up in hats and scarves and we took the bus into town. Punters holding plastic pint glasses spilled out of bars and on to the streets to catch a glimpse of

Clinton switching on the Christmas tree lights outside City Hall. We had burgers and chips in the Wimpy and muscled our way through the crowd as Van Morrison and Brian Kennedy sang 'Days Like This'. Then the president came on stage and there wasn't a sound as he told us how America would stand with us as we took risks for peace. Mummy pulled her mink coat around me and Toni. She smelt of Giorgio Beverly Hills and my belly was full of fried things, and everything was good in our world.

9

My father, the 'RA man

1997

Well, that lasted all of five minutes. Little over a year after Clinton's visit, the IRA exploded a lorry bomb in Canary Wharf, which is a pretty definitive way of saying, 'screw yer ceasefire, lads'. Not that things had ever really changed. For those missing their daily dose of tension, there was still the Twelfth to look forward to. For two consecutive years, Catholics living in Portadown had managed to stop the Orange Order from marching its traditional route to Drumcree church along the predominantly nationalist Garvaghy Road. But in the summer of '97, all hell broke loose when the RUC locked down the area to allow the Orange parade to pass through. Catholics across Northern Ireland took to the streets, and once again we made headlines around the world.

It looked like we were destined to return to the good old stop-and-search days. When she was seventeen, Mummy was on her way home, carrying a 5-foot fluorescent light tube. A soldier ordered her to remove it from its packaging. Mummy refused. 'You can see exactly what it is without me having to open it.'

The squaddie inched closer. 'Unless I see inside that box, you're not going anywhere.'

'Suits me.'

'For the love of God, do what you're told and stop holding everyone up.' Mummy turned round. Grandma was standing in the queue behind her, eyeballs heavenward. Although my parents had just started going out, incurring the disapproval of her new boyfriend's mother was a risk Mummy was prepared to take. She turned back the way she came and made it home without incident via the security gates leading to east Belfast, a mainly loyalist part of town. I guess Protestants bearing light fittings were deemed less of a threat.

We needn't have worried. The IRA announced another ceasefire shortly after Drumcree. Though later that year, dissident 'RA members formed the Real IRA. For the uninitiated, the Real IRA wasn't actually the *real* IRA. That was the Provisional IRA. Not to be confused with the Continuity IRA or the Irish National Liberation Army (INLA). It's hard to keep up. All you need to know is there was nothing new in the central theses of all these breakaway groups. It was the same old mantra – Brits out, our day will come, etc. Which is why, despite the ceasefires and Clinton coming to town, it all felt very much business as usual.

Elsewhere, life was changing at a dizzying pace. We had a new prime minister, for one thing. My parents approved. They thought Tony Blair would be good for

Northern Ireland. Shame about the annoying wife, but sure you can't have everything. And Forestside Shopping Centre opened, with Belfast's first ever Sainsbury's. There was an optimism to the 1990s, the decade – kicking off with the end of the Cold War – that took a gap year from history. Apartheid in South Africa ended, everyone was getting online (secure in the knowledge that a troll was nothing but a small creature in Scandinavian folklore), and the Spice Girls, with their big shoes and even bigger dreams, made everything – from feminism to female friendship – seem gloriously uncomplicated.

Not that it was all Buffalos and world peace. Wars were still waged. Tragedies continued to happen. We were visiting Hil with Bernie and her kids – Hil had just moved to Cambridge – when Princess Diana died. It had been a strange weekend. Hil was upset because the other mums on the estate were less than impressed with her twenty-year-old Czech au pair, who insisted on walking the kids to school in denim hot pants, and Uncle Brendan was annoyed that we got lost en route to theirs and arrived three hours late, which resulted in him burning the barbecue. Mummy said she thought burnt meat was the point of barbecues, which made my uncle even more irate.

So the mood was already strained when Hil woke us up early on the Sunday morning to tell us Diana had been killed in a car crash. We were all a bit subdued driving back to Liverpool later that day to catch the ferry home, because whatever you thought of Diana and the monarchy, it was sad. My family didn't have a huge issue with the British royal family. I know we were meant to loathe everything they stood for, and we supported elected Sinn Féin MPs in their decision not to take their seats in Westminster (they refused to swear an oath of allegiance to the queen). Secretly, I think Mummy admired Elizabeth II – the unwavering sense of duty, the filial loyalty.

We docked at Belfast Harbour the next morning and Mummy drove us straight to school. Everyone was talking about Diana, the tragedy eclipsing our all-important post-summer catch-ups. As the week went on, all my classmates had something to say about the massive outpouring of grief in England. The majority thought it was excessive – the collective madness, people calling in sick to work because they were heartbroken over losing someone they never met. I could see where my classmates were coming from. There were girls in my year who'd lost people they loved, through the Troubles or life in general, and they still managed to get up every day, brush their teeth, get the fake tan on. At the same time, there seemed something liberating about emoting. Seeing others talk about their feelings openly, without fear of being told to wise up. That English stiff upper lip had started to quiver. People now had a licence to express themselves. In Britain anyway.

It was a big year for Toni and me. My sister was starting St Dominic's and at fourteen I was entering my fourth year. Finally, I'd get to wear the shin-length, tartan pleated kilt reserved for the senior-school girls. As with everything else in Belfast, the skirt bitterly divided opinion. There were those like Auntie Hil, who, during her time at St Dominic's, wore her tartan with pride, saw it as a symbol of womanhood, the childishness of junior school firmly behind her. Bernie, on the other hand, was convinced it was her hatred of the skirt that led her to drop out of school before finishing her exams. She couldn't stand looking at it another day. The current school board appeared to fall into Bernie's camp, ditching the tartan in favour of a more sombre maroon A-line design. Mel was thrilled. Unlike its predecessor, you could roll it up at the waist to skim the crotch, a move swiftly overturned by Sister Frances whenever she passed us in the corridor.

I had more pressing concerns than fashion on my mind. It was the first year of our GCSEs. I'd like to say I had my pick of subjects to choose from, but a score of 26 per cent in chemistry in the end-of-year exams precluded any chance of a career in science. Nor was there a bright future ahead of me in cartography. When asked by Sister Malachy to identify Cork on an all-Ireland map, I pointed to Dublin. (Having latterly consulted friends from Ireland's second city, the 'People's Republic', there is no greater crime.) So geography was out. That left drama and languages. Mrs Gough regularly accused me of showing off in French class – at our school, this meant you had potential. I reluctantly kept on German as well. I'd wanted to study Italian, but Mummy and Daddy Devlin had other ideas. 'German is the language of the future,' my grandfather told me when I complained to him about Mummy's meddling in my academic affairs.

My lack of autonomy was becoming an increasing

bone of contention at home. Following a row with Mummy over shaving my legs – 'Hair is there for a reason, Alix!' – I shoved a toothbrush and six pairs of socks into a plastic bag (I was going for maximum drama and figured a more considered approach to packing would lessen the impact) and moved in with Bernie, arriving home three hours later to watch the final episode of *ER*'s series three as Bernie didn't care for the medical drama.

Our relationship hadn't always been this tumultuous. As a child, I loved spending time with my mother, especially the sick days she encouraged us to take so we could eat oxtail soup on the sofa and watch Richard and Judy together. And when Daddy went away on business trips we'd get into her bed and she'd make up stories. A highlight was The Farting King, a series of tales about a flatulent monarch. Each instalment ended on a cliffhanger and we'd have to wait until the next time Daddy was away to find out who would 'plug the hole of the Farting King'.

Life with my mother was also unpredictable, thanks to her mercurial mood swings. I watched a documentary once about how blowfish inflate themselves to several times their normal size when threatened. That was Mummy. She was always rowing with Bernie when her baby sister lived at home. I hated seeing my aunt puffy-eyed after yet another argument. Bernie had a 9 p.m. curfew, which she habitually broke, sneaking out her bedroom window and down the drainpipe to go drinking with her boyfriend. I couldn't understand why Mummy was so hard on her. I never stopped to consider what it must have been like to raise two families. I'd probably have been a blowfish too. But when you're a teenager, there's no such thing as context.

So we fought, frequently and over nothing. I had a spot on my chin and asked Mummy if she could make me an appointment with Dr McAuley as it was clear I needed to go on acne medication. She suggested starting with a natural alternative. Tea tree oil would be less abrasive on the skin and there was also the fact that I didn't have acne to consider. The woman was clearly intent on ruining my life. 'Why do you hate me?' The next morning, I stomped into the kitchen, ready for round two. The breakfast bar had been laid out with every Clearasil product on the market. Mummy had nipped out to the garage after I'd gone to bed in a huff. She was standing with her back to the hob, making a pot of tea. I came up behind her and gave her a hug and she put her hand on top of mine, squeezing it hard. Then she told me to bugger off and get ready for school.

Daddy was easier to get on with then. He was less complicated, had a lighter touch to discipline. He wanted to be our confidant, the cool dad. When I went to university and briefly took up smoking, Daddy's approach was more effective than Mummy's meltdown. He took one look at my attempts to channel Kate Moss's signature insouciance and laughed in my face.

'You look like a dick, love.'

I never smoked again.

He'd done well for a boy from Andersonstown. In the eighties, he set up his own production company, directing and producing TV commercials, of which two, in particular, proved regional hits: 'Fred, there's no bread', an ad for Spar, which successfully conveyed the trauma of running out of baked goods, and one for Primark, with dancing elves singing about how the store could cater for all your festive needs. The ads were so well received, Daddy started getting notions and bought himself a second-hand Jag that did twelve miles to the gallon. After a few months driving it up and down the Falls to jeers of 'Catch yerself on, ya big bollox', he traded it in for a Toyota.

I guess it was understandable the man wanted to treat himself. You would too if you'd been mistaken for an IRA man for fifteen years. It started before I was born, when Daddy got done for speeding coming back from a camping trip in Donegal with Uncle John. Back then, the police came to your house with a summons, and on this occasion they visited my father under Army protection – standard protocol at the time for law enforcement entering Andytown. Under 'previous convictions', the summons said, 'guilty of membership of a proscribed organisation and armed robbery'. Daddy explained that he had no previous convictions, and was instructed to go down to the station with several forms of ID.

'Did it bother you, being accused of something you didn't do?' I asked him when he told me the story.

He shrugged. 'You get used to it. That Mother's Day we were pulled over by the Army got to me more because it upset your grandma.'

Over the years, on business trips to London and

Manchester, without fail, the minute Daddy stepped off the plane, he was pulled aside and asked for ID. On one occasion, he'd just landed in Manchester with a colleague and a client when he was stopped by two plain-clothes officers from the Greater Manchester Police and escorted to a small room.

'What's this about?' Daddy asked.

'Oh I think you know,' said the cop with the brown tie.

'Umm, nope. Sorry, lads, you'll have to give me a clue. I'll have a P, please, Bob!'

Brown Tie wasn't laughing. Daddy pulled out his Nokia to call his colleague and tell her to go on to the production studio without him.

'What's that you've got there, sir? Can I see that for a second?' Brown Tie's partner, a middle-aged man with yellowing teeth, reached for the phone and put it in his pocket. 'I'll just hold onto this for a while.'

The officers left Daddy in the spartan room. It was then he realised he was in a holding cell. After a while, they brought him into an interview room. Yellow Teeth pulled up a chair. 'So, sir, who is this Mr Cherry?'

My father drew a blank. 'I have no idea. Never heard of him.'

Brown Tie raised a polystyrene cup to his lips and took a long sip of his coffee. 'Well, he's very interested in you.'

Daddy started to sweat. Who was this mysterious Mr Cherry? Had he met him out one night when he was steamin'? It was possible. The wrap party for the 'Fred, there's no bread' shoot had been a rager.

It turned out Mr Cherry was a solicitor. Daddy's colleague had called Mummy. She immediately got the Devlin family firm onto the case, who instructed one of their lawyers, Mr Cherry, to deal with the matter.

Brown Tie and Yellow Teeth started asking Daddy questions, quickfire, like a round of *Mastermind*:

What are the full names of your siblings? Where did you go to school? Tell us every address you've ever lived at.

They let him go in the end, leading him into the arrivals hall without explanation or apology, though Mr Cherry got a letter seven months later from a detective chief inspector confirming that, though Daddy had the misfortune to share a name with a leading person of interest, he was not, in fact, a terrorist himself.

It was years before he risked travelling without that letter.

That November, we had a celebrity visitor. Just three weeks after her inauguration, Mary McAleese, president of Ireland and former St Dominic's head girl, arrived at the school. Sister Frances could barely contain her excitement. She organised a welcoming committee of her finest pupils, selecting Mel to play clarinet alongside a handful of other gifted students, including my sister, who formed a guard of honour for Mary outside the front steps.

Nat and I were deemed neither sufficiently gifted nor honourable to participate, which was probably a good thing, as we were too busy gaping at our classmates' attempts to get a photo – not with the first native of Northern Ireland and the second woman ever to serve as the Irish president, but with Gerry Adams, who for some reason was accompanying Mary with Secretary of State Mo Mowlam. 'Big Ger, over here!' Colleen shouted from the crowd, with the same demented enthusiasm usually reserved for a Backstreet Boy.

By far the biggest event that year was my first kiss. His name was Anto. I met him at Ashley, a parish disco organised by the parents of St Bride's, just off the Lisburn Road. He expressed a vague interest in lip action via Mel, who knew him from primary school, but nothing had come of it. (Perhaps this was because I said things like 'lip action'.) I wasn't ready for this significant milestone anyway. Even though I'd taped every episode of *My So-Called Life* and watched Claire Danes and Jared Leto snog a million times, I was terrified I wouldn't know what to do with my mouth when the time came. Also, Nat thought Anto looked a bit like Celine Dion and I couldn't get the image out of my head. Everyone at school had something to say about my lack of experience. 'For fuck's sake, you've built it up too much. It's a piece of piss once you get started. Just find a wee boy and stick the lips on him.' I appreciated the sound advice from Aisling and made up my mind to stick the lips on Anto the next time we met.

We got ready at Mel's house as she lived down the road from Ashley. I wore a waist chain around indigo bootcut Levi's, doused myself in Versace Red Jeans and stuck a tube of Boots Sugar Plum tinted lip balm in my back pocket for the big moment.

Mel wasted no time, marching up to Anto as soon as we arrived. 'Will you see my friend?'

'Sure.'

And it was that easy. We started snogging to cheers from Nat and Mel. 'MMMBop' came on and it was hard not to pull away and dance with the girls. Those Hanson boys were such lady-killers. I must have been amazing at the kissing, because one of the dads who was chaperoning, inexplicably wearing a full tux, felt compelled to intervene. 'Time for a commercial break, people.'

Afterwards, Anto asked if I wanted to go to see *Titanic* the following weekend. I thought a group activity would be an easier sell to Mummy and Daddy, so we agreed we should ask his friend Paul and my friend Kelly, who were at that moment feeling each other up in the cloakroom. For our date, I settled on black jeans and a forest-green crop top, as close as I could get to the outfit Julia Roberts wears when chasing Michael in a bread van in *My Best Friend's Wedding*. Unfortunately, I wasn't blessed with Julia's physique and there was a bit of overspill (I put it down to the seven consecutive Bounties I ate at breaktime that Friday, the ultimate two-fingered salute to Mummy's no-confectionery rule) but Anto didn't seem to mind as we kissed the entire time Jack was painting Rose like one of his French girls. Sadly, I couldn't get Celine Dion out of my head and on the Monday I got Mel to call Anto and end our fledgling romance. He took it exceptionally well. Perhaps I wasn't as good a kisser as I'd thought.

I wasn't the only one romancing. Gogi was seeing

Angela, a leggy German he'd met on a skiing holiday in France. It came as a surprise when Mummy said there was someone new on the scene. He'd been going with Gillian for a while, though things had started to go downhill after she scratched her name on a window of the Connemara cottage with a diamond ring, a present from Gogi. She said she wanted to check if it was real.

The weekend we first met Angela, Daddy Devlin made himself scare. He was used to Gogi's girlfriends coming and going over the years and they always kept a respectful distance. Perhaps Gogi gave Angela the impression he had taken the old man in as an act of duty, because she wasted no time in making herself at home. Toni and I were sprawled in front of *Blossom* when she appeared, a 6-foot blonde in shoulder pads you could have balanced wine glasses on. Angela switched on the big light – 'Es ist too dark in here!' – then planted herself on the sofa behind us. After five minutes watching Blossom and Six freak out over a rumour that Blossom went all the way with Dennis at the multiplex, she got up, said, 'This is a very silly show' and left.

We got used to this abruptness over time, and while you wouldn't exactly describe the relationship we had with Angela as warm, she was grand, and I think she liked us. When I unintentionally lost a bit of weight after realising seven Bounties a day was unsustainable, she nodded in approval. 'Alix, you have shed your pig ham.' I spoke the occasional bit of German with her – nothing beyond asking for directions to the train station – and she seemed to appreciate the effort. Maybe that's what Daddy Devlin was alluding to when he said German would be the language of the future. Gogi's future.

Angela lived in Kitzbühel, a chocolate-box pretty Alpine town in the Austrian Alps. Gogi took Toni and me there one weekend for a skiing trip. Her apartment smelt of fresh laundry and almond butter cookies, which she made for our arrival. There was a softness to Angela in her natural habitat, and it was going well until I fumbled getting off the ski lift, stuck one of my poles in her crotch and she went flying into a mound of snow, spraining her leg. Gogi was furious – it was the first time he'd shouted at one of us and that's when I knew Angela wasn't just another one of his glamazons.

She moved to Belfast and in with Gogi and Daddy Devlin not long after that trip. There had been no consultation with my grandfather. She just turned up one day and started redecorating. I heard Mummy tell Daddy her brother was an arsehole, and in the middle of the night she shoved Daddy Devlin, the dogs and as many books and tins of mackerel as they could fit into the car, and moved him into Uncle John's house. John had moved out and was living in England, but had a place around the corner from Daddy Devlin and Gogi.

Two days later, Gogi and Angela turned up at ours enquiring where Daddy Devlin had gone. Mummy brought them into the front room. Toni and I tried to eavesdrop from the stairs, but we couldn't hear what was being said. And even though everyone was civil when they left, something was broken. That closeness between Mummy and my uncle wasn't there anymore. Months later, Mummy arrived at Uncle John's with dinner for Daddy Devlin, as she did every day. She found him on the floor of his room, foaming at the mouth. He was in hospital for nine months as he learned how to hold a teacup all over again. Our grandfather came to live with us after that.

10

Smells like teen spirit

Remember the scene in *Dangerous Minds* where ex-marine-turned-high-school-teacher Michelle Pfeiffer tells her students that there are no victims in her classroom?

'You have a choice. It may not be a choice you like, but it is a choice. You choose to get on that bus.'

My mother advised me that if I chose not to get on that bus to school, all holy hell would break loose.

It's fair to say my first few years at St Dominic's were emotional. I spent a good deal of time hiding out in the chapel, hoping Finoula Murphy wouldn't make good on her promise to 'knack [my] ballix in'. It wasn't just Finoula. When Dervla McKee wrote *Kelly and Pauline are dickheads* on the wall of a toilet cubicle after I had an argument with the girls (Dervla had gone to primary school with me and I was touched by her loyalty), Mrs Conlon gave me lines for inciting Dervla to vandalism. Auntie Bernie had had trouble with Mrs Conlon when she was at St Dominic's too, though Mummy says Bernie was mustard and had trouble with everyone. Another teacher told Mel off for looking at her in the eye when she was speaking to her. (I don't know where she was supposed to look, but it took me years to stop fixing my gaze on the floor whenever someone senior would address me.) I moaned at my mother incessantly for sending me to St Dominic's and begged her to find me another school. Eventually, she snapped. 'Alix, you got a C in your eleven-plus. I couldn't get you in anywhere else.'

Don't get me wrong. Academically speaking, St Dominic's was, and still is, an excellent school and I'd be hard pushed to get in with my C now (thanks, Mummy). And for all the talk of ballix-beatings, apart from the time Finoula pinned me to a wall and tugged on one of my wispy strands at the front, I remained physically intact during my seven years there.

The problem was me, or more specifically, my face. It had, seemingly overnight, transitioned, the inoffensive features of girlhood replaced by those of Isaac, the eldest Hanson brother. I say this without exaggeration or self-pity. Looking back over holiday snaps from that period recently, my dad exhaled through his teeth. 'Jesus, that's a face only a mother could love.'

I think this was less a recoiling at my train tracks and half-eyebrows, lost in an overly zealous plucking session, and more a meditation on my unwillingness to find joy in any activity that involved an uninterrupted fortnight in the company of my family. The evidence is damning – there's a picture of my parents and sister, laughing and eating gelato in front of the Leaning Tower of Pisa; another of Mummy hugging Minnie Mouse at Disney World. In every shot, I'm lurking in the background looking like someone who has just endured a colonoscopy.

It's the moisture of early adolescence that's the cruellest blow. Every part of my body perspired. This was particularly problematic at mass, when I'd offer a dripping palm to the unsuspecting stranger beside me and endure the horror of watching them wipe their hand on their trousers. It got to the stage where right before the priest said, 'Let us offer each other the sign of peace', I'd sprint out of the chapel.

Completing this triumvirate of humiliation was my uncle. Before I lost my pig ham, Gogi saw it as his duty to alert me to the unwelcome changes in my body. 'It's all about discipline, kiddo,' he'd say, pounding the treadmill in the games room in his tiny white squash shorts, his habitual Dunhill between his fingers. 'You need to cut out the shit and get your arse off the sofa.'

My thinking was, if I changed schools, my face might change with the move. Or maybe I'd change back into someone who didn't consider her face. It wasn't something to compare or prettify. It was just a face.

I didn't fit in my body, but I did feel at home in Mrs Watson's drama class. We lived for her lessons, to the detriment of our other subjects. We got detention for turning up late to German because we were rehearsing a play we wrote about a girl who takes ecstasy on the night of her GCSE results and dies. (We thought we ought to have been praised for the unequivocal 'Say no to drugs' message.) We got detention for turning up late to English because we were practising a murder mystery we wrote, in which I played sleuth Ophelia Landsbury

– I spent weeks watching Mummy's detective shows with her to help me fully inhabit the role. And I was so committed to my performance as Titania, queen of the fairies in our third-year production of *A Midsummer Night's Dream*, I stuffed my mother's wedding dress into my rucksack after she'd expressly told me not to take it, and left it on the bus on the way home.

Like Nat and me, Mel was keeping drama on for GCSE, which put the three of us in the same form class for the first time. I was happy with this new arrangement. Far from being a threat to my friendship with Nat, Mel and I had become mates in our own right. We enjoyed the same books, spent the majority of our time talking about food – what we'd just consumed, when we'd eat again, which Findus Crispy Pancake filling was the best – and Mel had also been told she resembled a Hanson brother, though she drew the long straw: Taylor was the more feminine of the trio. The day Mel and I properly bonded was when she suggested we skip English Lit. I'd never bunked off school before, other than the sick days Mummy encouraged us to take when we were younger. Mel and I snuck out the front gates, making our way furtively along side streets until we got to the Falls Library, where we were less likely to be spotted waiting on a taxi.

A brief word about west Belfast taxis, for no story about growing up on the Falls is complete without them. You know the iconic London black cab? The west Belfast taxi looks the same, only during the Troubles, they weren't available for private hire. Think of them more as a bus service, collecting passengers en route to a predetermined destination. You could say we were early adopters of the Uber Pool, which is probably the only time you'll hear Belfast described as an early adopter of anything. Cabs were flagged down in the street, and when you wanted the driver to pull over you rapped the window with a coin. When Falls residents started burning buses to use them as barricades against the Army in the early days of the conflict, bus drivers, understandably, refused to enter the area and we were left with no public transport system. Someone went over to London, bought a black cab and started their own bus service. Soon, others followed suit and the Falls Taxi Association was born.

The buses were more or less back up and running – though you still encountered burnt-out shells in the middle of the road – by the time I started at St Dominic's, but I still preferred getting a taxi home. Compared to 30p for the bus, the 50p fare was steep, but it was worth it to get back in time for *Neighbours*. The black taxi experience wasn't without its drawbacks. Reliably, someone would climb into the cab laden with plastic bags from their big shop at Curley's and ask you to do them a wee favour and hold the one with all the frozen goods on your knee. By the time you got home, your nether regions were numb. You might have the added misfortune of being sandwiched between two excessively large people. Or, if you sat on one of the pull-down seats, you spent the entire journey rapping on the window whenever one of your fellow passengers wanted to get out.

Mel and I got lucky and hailed an empty cab. We

bought a couple of chocolate muffins at Dunkin' Donuts, which had recently opened (first Sainsbury's, now the American multinational had arrived – the perks of peace), then went back to Mel's to binge-watch MTV's *The Real World*. Our absence was flagged to Mrs Conlon, who called our mothers to inform them of our truancy. Mummy told our year head she was appalled and would be having words when I got home, high-fiving me when I walked in the door that evening.

Mel and I agreed that when Mrs Conlon pulled us aside after assembly the next day, we'd hold our ground and under no circumstances apologise.

As predicted, the following morning our year head launched into a diatribe on honour and veritas. Hand on hip, skirt rolled up, Mel was true to her word, and when asked to explain herself, shrugged her shoulders.

Mel is so badass. I can't wait to stick it to the old bag.

Mrs Conlon turned to me. 'And what do you have to say for yourself, Miss O'Neill?'

I fixed my gaze on my pigeon toes. 'I'm so sorry, Miss. It'll never happen again.'

It happened again. We skipped Miss Rooney's history class with Nat and our new friend Niamh. The eldest of four girls, Niamh was an excellent cook and thought there was no problem in life that couldn't be made better with a good lasagne. Parents loved her – when she met Niamh for the first time, my mother said she'd entrust her with the keys to her house any day.

'Ugh. Parents are so stupid,' Nat fumed, finishing off a litre of White Lightning straight from the bottle. 'Niamh's a massive pisshead.'

Nat met Niamh through hockey club and invited her round to Mel's one night to share a spliff and listen to Denise and Johnny's *Especially for You*. Mel had bought the chart-topping single for Nat as a Christmas present, but decided she may as well get her money's worth before gifting it. The evening took a bad turn when Nat claimed she was hallucinating and threatened to call an ambulance unless Mel made her toast. Which, to Mel's credit, she did – before getting a taxi into town with Niamh and leaving Nat to whitey alone in her downstairs toilet.

The four of us had decided to go into town for lunch at my parents' pub. They'd bought Whites Tavern a few years previously. One of Belfast's oldest bars, it was tucked down an alleyway in the city centre. When the pub changed hands, my parents commissioned a huge stained-glass window featuring each of Ireland's four provinces for the new dining room. They spruced up the old flagstone floor and introduced a menu of traditional favourites. Their hope was that Whites would be popular with tourists, but Belfast in the early nineties was the last place you'd want to visit, and the punters never came. So instead my parents started up a gay night every Wednesday, which was a surprise hit. I worked there the odd night when I was fifteen. Too young to serve pints, I cleared glasses and cleaned the toilets, though after I walked in on an amorous couple pressed up against the hand dryer in the ladies, Mummy decided to put me on the early shift.

It was a risky move – venturing into the city centre for our illicit lunch instead of Spring Fry around the corner – and predictably invited jeers of 'snobby bastards'. We were undeterred. Sneaking around the back of the school, we thought we'd escaped undetected, when Niamh let out a cry.

'She's seen us!'

Miss Rooney was staring out the window of her classroom holding a blackboard duster. She looked like she wanted to chuck it at us. A small-boned woman with closely cropped curls and a thick west Belfast accent, Miss Rooney was the last person you wanted to get on the wrong side of. You'd be sitting in class discussing the Cuban Missile Crisis one minute and the next she was off on a rant about people living on the Malone Road not paying their taxes.

'Run!' Nat shouted as we tore out the back gates, crashing into a soldier on patrol, his rifle cradled across his body.

He tensed, eyes narrowing, and tightened the grip on his gun.

'Sorry!' cried Niamh. 'Our teacher's seen us on the beak and is going to kill us if she catches us.'

The soldier stared at us for a minute – he was probably trying to work out if we were smuggling any incendiary devices – then broke into a smile. 'On you go, girls. I won't tell.'

I was waiting on Nat in the toilets of McDonald's. We'd arranged to have a carryout – Belfast for 'pre-drinks' – in town as her friend Claire was visiting from Dublin for the weekend. Nat wanted to see if we could get into Lavrey's, a bar and club next door to the Golden Arches.

Over the phone at Nat's earlier that week, we'd agreed that Claire and I would share a half bottle of vodka and I volunteered to pick it up. The woman behind the counter in Winemark refused to serve me, so I accosted a student, who agreed to be my booze mule.

I arrived bang on time, though I knew Nat would be late. The girl didn't like to be rushed getting ready. Her showers were epic affairs, whereas I subscribed to Mummy's 'pits-and-bits' philosophy on personal hygiene. I kept myself occupied by rearranging the contents of my handbag. It contained a bottle of Body Shop White Musk spray and a fake ID. Pinned to the lining of my wallet was a miraculous medal. I found it in the drawer of Mummy's bedside table along with a crime thriller from the library, her knitting needles and a dog-eared photo of my grandmother. I wasn't sure if there was a patron saint of teenage drunks, but as my drinking career was in its infancy, I thought it would be good to have some divine protection onside. It did Moira no harm the time she and Mummy went back to ours after Auntie Bernie's wedding. Moira was on the vodka tonics. After an hour, it had barely touched the sides. On inspection of the bottle, they discovered she'd been drinking holy water. Mummy Devlin had gone to Knock (Graceland for Ireland's Catholics) a couple of years before she died and brought every vessel in the house with her.

After thirty minutes, I decided there was no harm in a capful of vodka. Five shots later, I was over my annoyance at the girls' tardiness. I'm not sure when they arrived. All I remember is looking up at Nat and

Claire, the latter puce with rage, waving an empty bottle of Smirnoff above my head.

In my defence, I'd yet to familiarise myself with the etiquette around helping yourself to someone else's carryout. I was new to the drinking game. The girls and I had started hanging out in the park next to Mel's house a few weeks previously with some of the boys from her old school. We'd wear Puffa jackets and pass around cans of cider. Everyone except PC got involved. Mel didn't recognise the oldest guy in the group, who stood at a distance from the rest of us, swilling from a bottle of Tesco Value Scotch. Rumour had it his initials stood for 'persecute Catholics', so we gave him a wide berth.

It was the only sensible decision we made during our early years on the sauce. We drank with all the abandon and arrogance of youth. We passed out in taxis, ventured to unfamiliar areas for the promise of a house party and were serial offenders in committing the mother of all friendship crimes – leaving the fallen behind in pursuit of a boy. Nothing existed beyond school and getting wasted at the weekend, not the politics on our doorstep or the distractions of the wider world.

The Good Friday Agreement had just been signed and I suppose we used the historic peace deal to justify our risk-taking. The weird thing about growing up in Northern Ireland was it didn't feel threatening – it felt like one of the safest places on earth. Even during the height of the Troubles crime in the region was the lowest in the UK, and in many places people would leave their doors unlocked at night. Obviously, we didn't score too hotly on the murder front and we loved a good carjacking, though such infractions were almost exclusively Troubles related. Mummy said it came as a shock when the conflict ended and ex-paramilitary members, unsure of their next step on the career ladder, started peddling drugs and money laundering. There could be no more excusing our sins away in the name of a greater cause. In that respect, we weren't all that different to anyone else.

It's hard to explain to someone on the outside how *normal* the abnormal seemed. A bomb scare didn't paralyse us with fear – it was an inconvenience, something that caused traffic jams and made you late for a hair appointment. In September 2017, when I was living in London, a device exploded on the Tube at Parsons Green. People were hurt, but thankfully no one was killed. In the grand scheme of terrorist atrocities carried out in the UK that year, it was small fry. Not according to a colleague who lived in Wandsworth, the next borough over. Arriving ten minutes late to the office where I was freelancing at the time, a takeaway coffee cup and half-eaten croissant in hand, you'd have thought she'd come from downtown Aleppo, the way she described her 'ordeal' getting into work.

'Ah, it was only a wee bomb in a Lidl bag,' I offered as a means of reassurance.

Another co-worker told me it was 'the most Belfast reaction' they'd ever heard.

If I'm honest, I resented my colleague for piggy-backing on someone else's pain. I imagined the response I'd get back home if I tried to elicit sympathy over something that had no impact on my life. *Catch yerself on. You're lucky you don't have it worse.* I ignored the impulse to share this sentiment and tried to be more understanding.

'That must have been scary. I hope you're okay,' I said.

My colleague had already turned her attentions to the latest celebrity gossip on the *Daily Mail's* sidebar of shame.

So yes, my friends and I drank with all the Bacchanalian vigour of a world without consequence, because we did feel lucky – lucky we weren't one of the families directly affected by the Troubles, lucky to be young and having a laugh.

Still, I was a reluctant drinker at first, unable to fully let go of the stuff of my childhood. I couldn't see the appeal of freezing my arse off on street corners when I could be sitting at home watching *Gladiators*. It unnerved me, the next stage. I wanted a bigger life, in theory – to travel, fall in love, live in Paris and smoke Gauloises at pavement cafés . . . But the reality of leaving Belfast and everything I knew was terrifying. We were sort of cut off in Northern Ireland. We knew our enemy, or we thought we did. *It's the Prods who are the problem. Stick with your own and you'll be fine. Never forget your roots.* That was the biggest crime – getting ideas above your station, losing sight of where you came from. Life beyond Belfast? Who knew what it would throw at you. Much as I pushed back at my mother for keeping us close, there was a comfort in being sheltered from adulthood. But you can't stay sheltered forever.

11

The Cres

The Crescent bar stood on the corner of Sandy Row, at the edge of the city centre. Officially, Sandy Row is in south Belfast, but you won't find a brunch spot or a beamer for miles. The area used to be the heartland of the Ulster Defence Association, a paramilitary group responsible for numerous attacks during the Troubles, including the brutal murder of a Protestant single mother of four. Ann Ogilby was beaten to death in a disused bakery by the organisation's women's unit, punishment for her affair with a married UDA commander. After being sentenced by a kangaroo court to a 'rompering' – a UDA term for torture followed by a fatal beating – Ogilby and her six-year-old daughter Sharlene were kidnapped by a group of UDA women. Sharlene was sent to a nearby shop to buy sweets while the unit's leader Elizabeth Douglas ordered two teenage girls to strike Ogilby repeatedly with bricks and sticks. On her return, Sharlene heard her mother's screams as she pleaded for her life.

Nearby Durham Street, the Catholic enclave where

Mummy lived until she was seven, was regularly targeted by Sandy Row UDA members in the early seventies, resulting in the deaths of four Catholics. In retaliation, a republican paramilitary group bombed the Crescent in 1974. Until 2012, visitors entering the area were greeted with a large UDA mural of a masked gunman alongside a warning to those in any doubt that they were entering loyalist Sandy Row.

There had never been a good time for a Catholic to venture into this unionist stronghold, but the summer I turned fifteen, tensions between the two communities were especially fraught. On 15 August 1998, four months after the Good Friday Agreement was signed, the Real IRA planted a car bomb in Omagh's town centre, killing twenty-nine people and injuring 220. One of the victims was a woman pregnant with twins. It was the single deadliest incident of the conflict, an act so heinous even the most hardcore republicans spoke out in condemnation of the IRA. The dissident group claimed they hadn't intended to kill civilians and declared a ceasefire, but the damage was done and any Catholic with an ounce of sense knew certain areas were now a no-go.

My friends and I did not fall into this camp. Everyone went to the Cres. It was legendary, a place where sectarianism was checked in with your coat at the front door. Local kids and affluent Protestants and Catholics from the suburbs got drunk together, we retched together, squeezed one another's body parts on the dancefloor rhythmically to 'Show Me Heaven'. We were a shining example of cross-community spirit, a rejection of the tribalism that had dominated our city for too long. Also, the Cres was the only pub that let in underage drinkers and served 70p shots.

Tommy Beattie, who has since passed (God rest him), owned the joint. An avuncular Protestant with big glasses and an even bigger laugh, he was a good friend of Gogi and Daddy Devlin's. You'd rarely see Tommy at the Cres, but his name above the door was enough to reassure middle-class Catholic parents that, despite its dubious location, the bar was one of the safest places their teenagers could be. Long before Daddy caught me with a Crescent stamp on my arm (I'd made it home and to bed without incident until I was snared getting a glass of water in the middle of the night), Gogi knew what the girls and I were up to.

One Saturday, he dropped Nat and me off with twenty quid in our pocket, more than enough to get us poleaxed, a portion of Bolognese chips in late-night takeaway Spuds, and a taxi home. Despite the cooling in Mummy's relationship with Gogi, Toni and I remained close to our uncle. It takes, on average, five hours and thirty-six minutes for a blowfish's metabolism to return to normal after it's been threatened. I figured it would take a human slightly longer to deflate and that Mummy's fury over Gogi moving Angela in would dissipate after a couple of months. No one can stay mad forever. Some blowfish get so tired from repeated puffing, they can't do it anymore.

Jimmy was the man you needed to impress to gain entry to the Cres, which wasn't hard – he'd set the bar remarkably low. As long as you were capable of standing in his presence and had some form of identification (I knew a guy who got in using his sister's driver's licence) you were all good. The 'Sawdust and soul' sign outside gave a taste of what was to come. Wood shavings, sticky with regurgitated alcopops, covered the floors and there were souls alright: bodies of the fallen piled up at the bottom of the staircase like a scene from Dante's *Inferno*. The toilets overflowed with apple schnapps-scented vomit and the alleyway out the back was an orgy of fingering and al fresco urination.

Nat's mum didn't realise the extent of the debauchery when she agreed to let her go to the Cres. She felt more comfortable with her daughter hanging out in Sandy Row than the Felons, a club on the Falls for former IRA prisoners where they made you stand for the Irish national anthem. My mother? She would have gone through me had she known where I was spending my Saturday nights. Around the time the girls and I started going out, Mummy was on the TV in her role as chairman of the Federation talking about the perils of underage drinking and the need for Belfast's bars to clamp down on baby-faced boozers.

Fortunately for me, she was too preoccupied to keep a close eye on what we were up to. After months insisting she didn't need help looking after my grandfather, she eventually agreed to a small team of carers coming in on rotation at night so she could get some sleep. Daddy Devlin had changed since the stroke. Frustrated at his inability to express himself the way he used to, he stopped trying to converse, committing to a passive existence in front of the TV. Daddy didn't

want to add to Mummy's stress by telling her I'd been
sneaking out to the Cres, and made a deal with me.
He said he'd keep quiet if I promised to stop drinking
until the start of my lower sixth year. I thought this
was highly sound of my father and eminently doable
on my part. I was adult, after all. I promised not to
touch a drop and I really did want to mean it.

'Someone chuck me over the SunShimmer.'

Mel is standing in the doorway to her bedroom in
a red miniskirt, limbs like Corinthian columns. She's
paranoid about her pale skin, but as I point out, she's
already been genetically blessed. We all have, to a certain
extent. Saoirse got the tiny waist, Nat the pert bum,
me the boobs. Mel is the legs of the group. Expecting
the ability to achieve a flawless tan on top of that is
just plain greedy. 'Give me a minute,' says Niamh,
squeezing a thick blob of brown liquid onto a tanning
mitt, the room filling with the smell of stale biscuits.

She slaps the mitt on Nat's back, rubbing vigorously,
then takes a good look at Mel. 'I'd ride ya.'

Mel beams. 'Aww, thanks, man. That's so lovely.'

Mel is hoping to make Adam jealous. They've scored
a few times, but things have cooled lately. We apply the
final touches of our make-up and head downstairs to
the taxi waiting outside, belting out 'Too Close'.

'Mel?' A voice calls from the study. Mel pretends not
to hear.

The way that you shake it on me
'Mel.'
Makes me want you so bad sex-u-alllyyyy, oh girl!

'Melina!'

Mel rolls her eyes. 'Yes, Dad?'

'What are you wearing?'

'It's just a skirt.'

'It's a belt. Go back upstairs and put something half decent on.'

Nat, Niamh and I leg it to the taxi. It's the same argument every week. Mel wears something risqué, her dad tells her to change, she argues back, then appears to capitulate only to stuff the offending item of clothing in her bag and change in the taxi.

We arrive at the Cres, fist-bump Jimmy, and take a lollipop from the bowl on the desk beside the cloak-room – toffee flavour this week. Heading straight to the bar, Mel gets in a round of sambuca shots for £2.80. Niamh calls her a flash bastard. After a brief lap of the place to scope out who's around, we spot Adam in the corner with his friends. He clocks Mel and his eyes widen when he sees The Red Skirt. We strut past all nonchalant like we haven't seen him, and he calls us over. The chat is strained at first, but after another few rounds of shots everyone is in flying form. Mid-conversation with Adam, Mel rolls off her chair and onto the floor, landing on her backside. She doesn't move, doesn't try to get up, she just sits there.

'Mel, get up off the floor,' says Nat.

At first, I think she's trying to ride it out to not make a big deal of falling so unceremoniously in front of Adam, but I don't think she realises she's not in her seat anymore as she continues her story right where she left off.

My head starts to spin. I leave the girls to it and make my way to the bathroom, the grim aftertaste of sambuca creeping up my throat. I stumble into the toilets and place my head against the mirror.

'Are you okay?' Fixing her bronzer beside me is a tiny girl with a close-cut black bob and big hazel eyes like a matryoshka doll. She's wearing a pink neon push-up bra under a white crop top.

'I don't feel goo—'

She holds my hair back as I hang over the sink. When I'm done, she sits me down on the floor beside the cubicles, then disappears, coming back five minutes later with a plastic pint glass of water. She places it next to me and takes a tube of toothpaste out of her bag, administering a blob onto her index finger and rubbing it around my gums.

'You'll be alright there for a while. Just sleep it off. I'm Jennifer, by the way.'

She disappears out the door in the direction of the dancefloor and into a mist of dry ice.

I'm woken by Nat. It's time to go home. Nat says no taxi will take us, the state I'm in, and her mum is going to freak out if we're not back by 1 a.m. I forgot I'm staying at hers tonight. Jennifer offers us a lift – her mum is coming to pick her up. All I remember from the car journey is Jennifer's mum asking if I'm okay and Jennifer telling her I had some bad prawns. I've never had a prawn in my life. Our family's take on seafood is a fish supper from Long's. This Jennifer is dead sophisticated.

I spend much of the next morning on the floor of

Nat's family bathroom. Not even the magnolia room spray can ease my suffering. When I manage to get my act together and make it home, Toni intercepts me at the door.

'Daddy knows.'

Shit. I walk in and try to act breezy. Mummy doesn't notice – she's cutting up liver and potatoes for Daddy Devlin – but Daddy shoots me a sad look and my hangover kicks in again.

And then there were five. As the Spice Girls were saying goodbye to Geri, we found the missing piece of our puzzle. A year older than the rest of us, Jennifer went to the same co-ed school where Mel had spent her first year. This proximity to boys gave her a worldliness desperately lacking in our group. We called her 'Mama'.

When not boozing, we'd hang out at Nat's, eating waffles and doing Beverley Callard's *Real Results* video to atone for the waffle eating. Beverley had left *Coronation Street* to focus on building her fitness empire. It was a loss to our weeknights. Mummy used to watch the soap all the time, though the Angry Northern Irish Person trope – Bev's frequently violent on-screen ex-husband Jim McDonald robbed a building society in a flat cap so she could buy the Rovers back from their son Steve – was beginning to wane.

Sprawled across cushions on the floor of Nat's living room, the top buttons of our combat trousers undone, Nat sucking on Scarfy – a rag from a childhood blanket – we were different with one another with no one else around. Relaxed. Unselfconscious. Not arseholes. When we were out, it was every woman for herself. Woe betide the friend who was too drunk to stand up and needed chaperoning (guilty), or who cornered you for a deep and meaningful when those first few beats of 'Superstar' started to play.

It's just as well I was enjoying my downtime with the girls. Since I'd broken my pact with Daddy, I was grounded, and hadn't set foot in the Crescent in weeks. It wasn't too bad, the not drinking. We were all behaving more responsibly and had even got ourselves jobs, motivated by a loose plan (conceived under the influence) to go to Magaluf for our sixth-form holiday. I'd never been abroad without adult supervision, so I knew I'd have to be on my best behaviour to convince my parents to let me go.

Jennifer had a job in the cookery section at Debenhams. She wasn't popular with her colleagues, for refusing to carry out routine checks for incendiary devices. If the store got a suspect call, but the bosses didn't feel an evacuation was necessary, the employees were sent to look for bombs inside teapots. Jennifer told her line manager she hadn't received adequate training for such matters and didn't even know what an incendiary device looked like. Besides, she wasn't getting paid enough to justify the risk.

Her boss told her to 'look for something with wires', and said that she obviously thought rooting out bombs was beneath her. 'You're no better than anyone else,' he scolded, adding that the worst that would happen was that she'd lose a few fingers.

She gave in – no one likes to be called a snob.

Mel and Nat were waitressing in town at a family restaurant, and Niamh and I spent two nights a week pulling pints in one of Mummy's family bars. One evening, Niamh gently tried to get one of the punters, a man in his fifties we hadn't seen before, to drink up as last orders had long been called. He'd been sitting alone at the end of the bar all night. He stood up slowly and took an uneasy step towards Niamh.

'You know what, love?' he slurred. 'You'd be surprised at what a couple of pounds of Semtex would do to this wee bar.'

He knocked back his Jameson, put on his coat and walked out the door.

Mummy and Daddy Devlin were in front of the TV when I got home, eating buttery slices of toasted Veda and watching *The Fugitive*.

'Is that you back, love?' Mummy called. 'Come watch with us.'

I took off my apron and gave my shirt a sniff. It smelt of chip fat and stale Guinness.

'I'm just going to have a shower first. Here, what's Semtex?'

Mummy took a bite of her malted toast as Tommy Lee Jones said he didn't care whether or not Harrison Ford had killed his wife.

'It's an explosive for making bombs,' she said, without taking her eyes off the screen. 'Why?'

'Oh. I met a man tonight in the bar. I think he wants to blow the place up.'

'Is that right? Ach, doesn't your heart go out to that Dr Richard Kimble.' She points at the TV and shakes her head. 'His wife was murdered by a one-armed man. Shockin' what goes on in the world. Come sit down.'

She lifted the blanket on her lap – a lemon candle-wick bedspread that had belonged to Mummy Devlin – and patted the sofa.

I sighed and climbed in beside her.

12

Rides and prejudice

1999

Let me lick you up and down til you say stop . . .
  'Oh my God, that Bobak is such a ride.'
  Let me play with your body, baby, make you real hot . . .
  'You know what? I quite fancy Dane.'
  Let me do all the things you want me to do . . .
  'What? Sort it out, man! I'd marry him, maybe, but for a shag it would totally be Mark.'
  Cause tonight, baby, I wanna get freaky with you.
  'I can't watch anymore. It's too hot.' Nat grabs the remote off Niamh and switches channel to *Countdown*. Nothing like an anagram to cool the loins. Though we all agree Carol Vorderman is looking seriously foxy these days. Excellent arse. She should win that Rear of the Year.
  I'm sixteen. The girls and I are meant to be rehearsing for our GCSE drama practical, but the Another Level boys, muttering sotto voce to camera about whipped cream and wanting to be our nasty man, have other

ideas. I'm not sure I do want a nasty man. Despite our endless conversations about sex, the only one actually having any is Jennifer, who's been going with Sam for a couple of months. I'm holding out on a boy who'll serenade me with a brass band like Heath Ledger does to Julia Stiles in *10 Things I Hate About You*. According to our English teacher, Miss Ramsey, the film is misogynistic as it's based on a Shakespeare play about crushing a woman's spirit. Colleen says Miss Ramsey is a feminist. I think I'll become a feminist too after I've found myself a boyfriend.

We've started kissing Methody boys. Methody is a rare thing in Belfast – an integrated, co-ed school, where all the well-to-do parents send their kids. Nat's been snogging Aidan, who told Niamh the night we all first met that he wanted to 'ride the Italian arse off her'.

'But you're not Italian,' I say to Nat.

She shrugs. 'There might be some Italian in my blood from way back. I tan really easily, man.'

Nothing fazes Nat. First, she's a British bastard and now her backside is other. It's a wonder she doesn't have identity issues.

Jennifer and Niamh are seeing Protestants. Niamh's Protestant Johnny plays hockey, as Protestants do, and Jennifer's one owns a bomber jacket that says 'If it's too loud, you're too old', and wears white jeans because he likes how they glow in the dark on the dancefloor of the Cres. He's a serious Prod, Sammy. His dad is an Orangeman and used to take Sammy on marches when he was little. When Sammy brought Jennifer home for the first time, he asked her if she was 'one of them'. Sammy says he has no interest in following in his dad's footsteps and taking up the orange sash. He's into trance and Jennifer, not divisive politics. Protestants can be sound when they want to be.

I think Mel is holding out for Robbie Williams. They have a connection, Robbie and Mel. We saw him at the Waterfront Hall the other week. I'm surprised Robbie came back to Northern Ireland, considering how he was treated last time Take That were here. The band's car was searched by the police and Mark said you could feel the tension in the air. Honestly, I despair of this place sometimes. As if the boys would try to blow up their own concert venue. They're lovers, not fighters.

Mel smuggled a quarter bottle of vodka down her knee-high boot and we managed to get right up to the front, where Rob could see us. Mel was convinced he was communing with her and we knew we had to meet him. Afterwards, we bumped into Joe, the manager of a restaurant Nat's family go to all the time for steak and tobacco onions. He was wearing a Take That T-shirt and growing what looked like an attempt at a Jason goatee.

'Did you enjoy the concert, girls?' he asked.

'It was amazing,' said Nat. 'Robbie serenaded Mel.'

'Ah, that's nice. You know he's staying next door at the Hilton?'

'Noooo!' Mel grabbed my arm to steady herself.

'Oh aye. Only, he's not checked in as Robbie Williams in case he's mobbed by fans. He's staying under a code name.'

Nat's eyes widened. 'What is it?'

Joe looked around, then leaned in and whispered in Nat's ear.

Nat nodded intently. 'Isn't that a girl's name?'

'I guess it throws people off the scent,' shrugged Joe.

Nat clapped her hands together. 'Amazing! Thanks, Joe – we owe you one!'

'No problem, girls. Keep 'er lit.'

We dashed across to the Hilton and marched up to reception.

'Hi there,' said Nat. 'We're here to see a friend, who's staying here. His name's Connie Lingus.'

The receptionist stared at us for a moment, then smiled. 'No problem. Give me a wee minute.' She started typing and stared at her screen. 'Hmmm. Nothing's coming up. Let me try "Lingus" first. Unusual wee name, isn't it?'

We had no luck at the Hilton – Joe must have been mistaken about the location, said Nat – so started calling around other hotels in the city centre until an irate manager came on the line.

'Who is this? You think you're funny, do you?'

'I don't understand,' said Mel, as we climbed into the back seat of Nat's mum's car twenty minutes later. 'Why were people freaking out? Do you think they were worried everyone had discovered Robbie was Connie Lingus?'

'Maybe,' said Nat. 'Connie Lingus. C-o-n-n-i-e L-i-n-g-u-s. It's an unusual one alright. Do you think Lingus is an English surname?'

'Girls!' Nat's mum was staring at us in the rear-view

mirror, mouth gaping like a salmon. 'Stop saying that word.'

The next day at school, Colleen informed us that 'Lingus' is most assuredly not an English surname. It was ages before Nat had steak and tobacco onions again.

I didn't know many non-Catholics when I was a kid. There was Cynthia, the wee Chinese girl from primary school, and that was pretty much it for ethnic diversity. Catholic Ireland wasn't exactly a cultural melting pot. Every Lent, charity boxes were sent to every household in the country to raise money for the 'black babies' and no one batted an eyelid.

As for friends on the other side, there was Tommy Beattie, who owned the Cres, and Daddy worked with a good few Protestants. Like Daddy Devlin, he changed his name when he started out in advertising in the eighties. 'Micky' sounded too Catholic, so for a while he went by 'Mike'. Until one day, he got fed up pretending and when a colleague was introducing him to a prospective client, he stopped him. 'You know what? It's Micky actually.'

After Big Sean, Greig was our favourite of Daddy's friends. He was gay as well as being Protestant, so that was two points for diversity. Greig had limbs the length of a sequoia tree and owned more designer glasses than Mummy did Downtown Radio mugs. Daddy loved to tell the story about the time he and Greig shared a hotel room on a work trip to Dublin and Greig said Daddy looked great in his Calvin Klein and chased him around the room, whipping him on the backside with a towel. Greig said it was just a bit of fun and that my dad isn't his type. Daddy moped around the house for days after that. He loved to be loved by everyone, my father, regardless of sexual orientation. Mummy eventually told him to get a grip – 'You're no goat's toe, Micky.'*

Greig came to all our parties. On one of Daddy's birthdays, he arrived with a tin of hash with Our Lady on the front and asked Toni, who was twelve at the time, to roll him a spliff, which Mummy wasn't too happy about. He also had a habit of getting his penis out. At my parents' annual St Patrick's Day do he showed his lad to Auntie Hil's mother-in-law, a no-nonsense retired nurse from Saintfield, a village out the country.

She took one look at it and said, 'Son, I've washed bigger', then resumed her conversation with my great-aunt Lily about how the price of mass cards has risen something shocking.

Mummy said Greig's compulsion to expose himself wasn't a Protestant thing or a gay thing. It was a Greig thing.

Everyone loved Greig, especially old women. They'd never met anyone so unashamedly themselves. You wouldn't have described the LGBT scene in 1990s Belfast as hopping, which is probably why the gay night at my parents' bar took off the way it did. Right up

---

* Another one of my grandmother's sayings. I suppose the closest definition is 'God's gift'. Note, you can't *be* a goat's toe. You can just *not* be one.

until the eighties, gay sex in the region was only legal at twenty-one (former DUP leader Ian Paisley's pledge to 'Save Ulster from Sodomy' back in the seventies didn't quite go to plan – the campaign only served to bring Protestants and Catholics closer together, the handful of gay venues in the region being one of the only shared spaces for the two communities), and the first Pride parade in Belfast didn't take place until 1991, eight years after Dublin and with just 100 people in attendance. I heard the organisers had to bring a rainbow banner up from the Irish capital as they didn't have one. Odd, considering our fondness for a flag.

Stuff we believed about Protestants:

- Their eyes were closer together than ours.
- They wore hats to 'church' (it was never mass).
- They were cleaner than us – Mummy was always saying, 'Now that's more Protestant looking' after a tidy-up.
- They kept their eggs in the cupboard, not the fridge.

A way of determining which community someone hailed from was by asking them if they were a 'Plate' or a 'Cup' (P for Protestant, C for Catholic – there was nothing sophisticated about our prejudice). Or you could get them to recite the alphabet. Everyone knew Protestants dropped their h's. More often than not, 'What school did you go to?' was the easiest way to establish whether you were talking to a potential friend or foe. If you were born in Northern Ireland before the Good Friday Agreement, chances are you've carried this guardedness with you throughout life. Keep your cards close to your chest, always be the one to ask the questions. It's no wonder I ended up a journalist.

There's a scene in *Derry Girls* where the pupils from Our Lady Immaculate are forced to take part in a cross-community exchange with boys from a local Protestant school. Father Peter asks the groups to list similarities between Catholics and Protestants. All they can come up with are differences – how Catholics are big into Abba and keep coal in the bath, and Protestants love soup and wear gilets (that one's actually true. All the Protestant lads we hung about with enjoyed a sleeveless padded jacket). It was wild, the prejudices we held about each other. Deep down, we knew we were more alike than we cared to let on, but it was drilled into us from an early age, the need to be vigilant around the other side.

When I was nineteen, I brought an English friend home from university for my birthday weekend. It was the twelfth of July and after a day's drinking in my parents' back garden, we decided to go in search of dancing and boys. I knew town would be dead, so called a taxi and asked the driver to take us somewhere with a bit of buzz. He brought us to a bar in Newtownards, a town as 'black as yer boot' in County Down. ('Black' was how my mother's generation referred to majority Protestant areas.) The pub was buzzing alright – with Orangemen toasting a successful

Twelfth. I got chatting to one at the bar after admiring his Lambeg drum and invited him and his friends to join us. At that moment, my father texted to see where we were and what we fancied for dinner.

I told my new friend I'd be right with him, and pinged Daddy back a message: *Won't be home for tea. Having a lovely time with the Orangemen and their big drums. Lots of love XX*

Daddy replied instantly. *What?! Where are you?*

In Newtownards with all the lovely Protestants. They're not that bad actually. Peace. XX

Sweet Jesus, Alix!! Which pub are you in? Leave immediately! Don't talk to anyone! I'm coming to pick you up.

Thirty minutes later, my father was outside and bundled us into his Saab. An overreaction? Maybe. This was 2002, three years into the DUP and Sinn Féin power-sharing executive. Technically, we were at peace, which is what I told Daddy when he gave out to me over breakfast the next morning.

'Talk some sense into your daughter,' he urged Mummy. 'I need a smoke.'

Of course, Daddy's take on our outing was coloured by long-held prejudices, and there's always a chance that that particular group of Orangemen would have accepted a Falls Road girl in their midst. Looking back, older and sober, I'm relieved I didn't stay long enough to find out. I reckon most Protestants would feel the same about strolling into a GAA★ club in west Belfast on a significant date in the republican calendar. Even

---

★ Gaelic Athletic Association.

now. Centuries of mutual mistrust aren't wiped out just because a couple of politicians sign a piece of paper.

The girls at school called us 'hun' lovers, a regional insult for a Protestant, because we hung out in town with unknown quantities and not on the Falls with our own kind. I don't think our classmates found our disinterest in republicanism offensive. They seemed to enjoy hearing tales of our Saturday nights sharing shots and saliva with Protestant boys.

I wasn't sharing anything with any Protestants. In fact, since Anto, my love life had been a non-starter. I'd kissed other boys, though no relationship could live up to the union between Melissa Joan Hart (also known as Sabrina the Teenage Witch) and Adrian Grenier in *Drive Me Crazy*, which at the time I considered to be the apotheosis of romantic love. Arguably, the film was one of the less memorable teen romcoms in a year that spawned some absolute classics such as *She's All That* and *Never Been Kissed* (both slightly problematic when revisited in your mid-thirties and a post #MeToo world) but there was something about the girl-falls-for-boy-next-door thing I couldn't resist. Sadly, I had no boy next door, cute or otherwise – we lived beside a convent for retired nuns.

I had two major crushes during my teen years. The son of an esteemed Catholic journalist who was frequently on the radio giving his hot take on the Troubles, Laurie was a less serious soul, big of hair and crumpled of shirt. He didn't say much the night we scored for the first time, but he did buy me a Pineapple Bacardi Breezer, which happened to be my favourite flavour, and this was everything. He *got* me. For the rest of the year we'd kiss intermittently when we bumped into each other on nights out. Although our non-physical interactions were limited, I convinced myself there was a deeper connection between us. Mel agreed and said the only reason Laurie hadn't asked me to be his girlfriend was because he was scared of the intensity of his feelings. Niamh disputed this logic and said that if a boy was into you, you'd know.

I was conflicted, and decided to talk to Mummy about it. Normally, Toni and I went to Daddy with this kind of thing – our mother didn't do affairs of the heart – but he was away on business. As predicted, she couldn't offer any insight into whether or not Laurie genuinely liked me, but she did suggest we drive past his house and see if we could spot him through the window, for the craic.

'Are you mad? What if sees us? He'll think I'm a stalker.'

She'd already thought of that, and produced two pairs of sunglasses and a couple of wigs from her collection (she was really into hair). We didn't catch a glimpse of Laurie. After driving up and down his street several times, we eventually admitted defeat and went home, stopping for a pastie supper (a Belfast classic – battered sausage, and potato fried in crispy batter) en route. It was the best fun I'd had with my mother in a long time.

Much as I fancied Laurie, he came a distant second to the true object of my affections. I met Ryan through his sister Lisa when I was thirteen, before Angela arrived on the scene. Their dad was friends with Gogi and the family and lived down the lane from my uncle. Ryan was ginger and in the year above me, and was the first boy I wasn't related to that I'd exchanged any meaningful conversation with. Like the time I was getting a glass of water in his kitchen and he asked me if I liked 'Pinball Wizard' and I said, 'Who?' And he said, 'Exactly! The Who', and seemed impressed.

My infatuation intensified on a ski trip to Courchevel. We went with Gogi and the families of some of his friends, fellow west Belfast lads, who, like my uncle, had moved out of the area when they started doing well for themselves. It seemed so glamourous, hitting the slopes for a week – and so alien. I couldn't get over the confidence of the other girls on the trip. They went make-up-free in the presence of the opposite sex and didn't care that their feet stank after a day in thick socks and ski boots. I'd notice this same confidence among the well-off English crowd I'd go on to meet at university. Where I came from, you got a new outfit for Christmas Day, Boxing Day, Easter and pretty much every high day and holiday in between. There was a pride in being new and shiny. Not for my privately educated peers. They wore their privilege in their dishevelment, moth-eaten cashmere jumpers and unbrushed hair the order of the day. No one gave me a heads-up on this artfully choreographed scruffiness and I wanted to impress Ryan, so I convinced Mummy to let me raid Miss Selfridge for essential après-ski outfits before we left, while Toni worked on her slalom at the dry slope at Craigavon.

As we ate in most nights on the trip, there was only one opportunity to dress up the entire week. The adults had booked a Michelin-starred restaurant, leaving the rest of us to fend for ourselves. Ryan's older brother said he'd take us out for fondue. I took my time getting ready. After much debate, I settled on a long black skirt in a magnolia pattern with a slit up one side, and a block heel mule, examining myself in the mirror. Aside from the train tracks, I was looking pretty sharp.

'Allie, what's taking you so long?' My sister barged into the room we were sharing and stopped when she saw me painting my toenails with the lavender varnish I got free in *J-17* that month. 'Erm, you know we're just going out for melted cheese, right? And are you seriously not wearing any tights? It's Baltic outside.'

I dismissed her the way I'd always dismissed my sister, convinced that my two-and-a-half-year head start in life gave me an urbanity beyond her grasp.

'You're too young to get it,' I told her. 'It's like Cher says in *Clueless* – "Sometimes, you have to show a little skin."'

Everyone was in the living room of the chalet dressed in fleeces and jeans when I walked in. Ryan's friend (whose name I kept forgetting because I didn't want to have his babies. We'll go with "Yer Man Jamie") looked up, slack-jawed. 'You do realise it's minus 3 outside?'

What was with the constant weather updates? All the girls fancied Yer Man Jamie. If you're into a strong jawline and facial symmetry, he was attractive, but he was no Ryan, who at that moment was explaining to my sister the finer details of pyroflatulence. Yer Man Jamie nudged his friend. Ryan looked over and raised a red eyebrow. My cheeks started to burn. I had two choices: I could go back upstairs to change and look like a complete idiot, or I could own my sartorial choices and introduce a new kind of après-ski style to this town.

It took Toni and me half an hour to complete the ten-minute walk to the restaurant. At first, Ryan and Yer Man Jamie took it in turns to help me back up each time I skidded on the ice in my heels, but after the sixth tumble they gave up and went on ahead with the others. My sister puffed out her cheeks and muttered something about the slit in my skirt and a frostbitten vagina, but she stayed with me. When we got to the restaurant, I fled straight to the bathroom to dislodge a thick lump of snow that had made its way into my pants, and sat with my feet under the hand dryer until the blood returned to my toes. I spent the rest of the evening trying to get Ryan's attention by dipping my skewer into the cheese pot in a suggestive manner that would leave him in no doubt about my feelings. Ryan failed to notice and I went to bed that night unkissed and picking gruyère out of my braces.

I returned home deflated, but not defeated. I was determined to make Ryan fall for me. And what better way of securing his affections than finding out what he was into. I needed to do a bit of reconnaissance. One afternoon, I borrowed Daddy Devlin's binoculars – he was a keen ornithologist – and decamped to the tree in the grounds of the nursing home beside Ryan's house. I'd hoped to catch a glimpse of him in his natural habitat, but one of the residents' dogs started barking up the tree at me and I was afraid of drawing too much attention to myself.

The calls started soon afterwards. Every Friday night for a month, I'd phone Ryan at his house under the pseudonym Rebecca. I'd always liked the name. Rebecca sounded like the kind of girl who had her shit together. (I'd yet to read the Daphne de Maurier classic of the same name, so was unfamiliar with the more sinister connotations of my new alias.) After a while, I roped Nat in, the pair of us squeezing into the phone box outside the Ashleigh disco, my stomach somersaulting as I dialled Ryan's number. I never stayed on the line long enough for Ryan to uncover my identity, and from what I can remember, the content of the calls was always complimentary – things like, 'I want to have your ginger offspring' – but when Ryan threatened to call the police, Nat told me I needed to pack it in.

I appreciate now that these attempts at getting to know Ryan better were a gross violation of his privacy and there is nothing charming or amusing about harass-ment, but I was young and in lust, and this was long before the Protection of Freedoms Act that made stalking a specific crime.

At the height of my obsession, I even wrote a song about Ryan. I needed an outlet for my pain and came up with a jazzy number, which I performed for the class one rainy breaktime.

Ryan, you got me cryin', I feel like dyin', oooooh
  Ryan
Ryan, your hair is red, let's go to bed
And we'll have sex, you've got such great pecs
We'll use a whip and handcuffs too
Oh Ryan, I need yooooouuu.

Silence.

Thirty pairs of eyes stared back at me. Maybe I'd gone too far with the interpretative dance moves. Whipping is graphic enough without the added visual.

Then Aisling started to laugh and the rest of class joined in. 'I knew you were a dirty wee bitch,' she said, slapping me on the back.

After that, everyone at school took an interest in my love life, cheering me on in my endeavours with Ryan. I'd never got on so well with my classmates. I realised there was a gain in making people laugh, in playing the clown. If you take the piss out of yourself, no one else will.

Before we knew it, it was the end of our fifth year. I didn't see much of Ryan that summer. Everyone was on holiday and the Cres was eerily quiet without its usual school crowd. One night in August, we decided to go to Lavrey's for a change. It was a good call. Shortly before midnight, Sam ran up to us on the dancefloor. We didn't see him at first. 'Superstar' was playing and the five of us were lost. This was *our* song, the only track that could make us dance for us, not perform for a group of lads. We didn't care who was watching or how our arses looked from the bar as we wrapped our spaghetti-strapped arms around one another. No one could penetrate this phalanx of love and drunkenness. Not Ryan. Not Mark from Another Level.

Sammy had to muscle his way through our circle. Jennifer's face dropped as he cupped a hand over her ear. 'What?!' There had been a shooting at the Cres. Masked gunmen had burst into the bar, shut the music off and warned all the Catholics they had five minutes to clear out. We dashed across the road to find out what was happening.

Jimmy stood at the door, refusing to let anyone in. 'Time to go home, girls.' He said it like he knew it was the beginning of the end for the Cres.

We laughed and told him we'd see him the following week. The pub was demolished not long after that, as we were entering our penultimate year at St Dominic's. A modern-day Cassandra was Jimmy.

It was the end of an era, not just for those who'd left behind a little part of their childhood beneath the rubble of the Cres, but for Northern Ireland too. After twenty-six years, direct rule in the region officially ended on 2 December 1999. We were masters of our own destiny again. Soon, it was the end of the millennium. We celebrated the arrival of Y2K at the Eg, a bar popular with students from nearby Queen's University. There was no sawdust on the floors – the Eg's clientele was classy enough to do its vomiting in the toilets.

The night had been an anticlimax. I couldn't find anyone for the countdown, and the DJ refused to play 'Superstar'. Midnight came and went, and for all the talk of the millennium bug, nothing happened. Everything was as it had been, we were still us. Maybe that wasn't such a bad thing. 'Let's go back to mine for waffles and Care Bears,' said Nat when I eventually found the girls. And we did.

13

Don't mess with our fake tan

There are those who claim their teenage years were their best years. A time when they learnt fundamental truths about life, love, themselves. When they forged the person they would become. I think we can all agree I am not one of these people. Had my adolescence been a training ground for adulthood, I'd currently be in rehab – or on Tinder's most unwanted list.

I'm glad I saw out these dark years in the nineties. I don't envy today's seventeen-year-olds. Imagine your every move, the drunken indiscretions, the navel gazing, the essential horror of your very existence, all caught on camera and immortalised on social media for the perverse enjoyment of others. I thank the sweet lord every day smartphones weren't around when the girls and I gave an inebriated yet earnest performance of 'Daddy Draws Me Naked', an original score, inspired by one of my father's art college sketches.

We were having a carryout in my front room when my parents were away one weekend. Niamh spotted the framed drawing on the wall.

'Lix, is that you?'

'Dude. My dad drew that. She was a model in one of his life drawing classes.'

'Huh. It looks like you.'

'Gross. She's naked!'

Mel put her Smirnoff Ice on the coffee table and walked over to the hi-fi beside the piano. Turning down the volume on the Vengaboys, she stretched her fingers flamboyantly and sat down at the keyboard. She tested several chords, inviting a respectful hush from the room, and cleared her throat.

Daddy draws me naked, oh yes he does.
You might think creepy, but it's arrrrrrrrrrt.

The five of us composed a chorus and two whole verses about the inner conflict between adhering to societal norms and living one's creative truth. We thought it was a masterpiece.

There is, however, one perk of modern adolescence I wish I'd had the benefit of. It's not easy asking someone out via any medium, but at least Generation Z have the luxury of the written word to hide behind. They can spend time constructing the perfectly breezy message. I remain convinced that had I been able to communicate my feelings for Ryan via WhatsApp, I'd have appeared sexy and mysterious instead of unhinged. Yes, we could text on our trusty Nokia 3310s, but this was reserved solely for the practicalities of meeting up. Weightier concerns – like asking someone to your school formal – demanded picking up the phone and having an actual conversation.

I had decided to ask Laurie to be my date to the biggest night in the St Dominic's sixth-form calendar, as Ryan was getting dangerously close to uncovering the identity of his anonymous caller. (He asked Nat at the Crescent one night if she was Rebecca. 'But Nat has a southern accent – you don't. He's not the sharpest, is he?' said Mummy when I told her we needed to circle the wagons. Asking Laurie to the formal would throw Ryan off the scent. To be fair to Ryan, no one watched as many detective shows as my mother did. Even Poirot took his time getting to the truth.)

Not that Laurie was a consolation prize. Although we hadn't kissed in a couple of months, I continued to delude myself that there was something beautiful and profound between us and if we had an opportunity to get to know each other better, he'd realise that he was my Pacey and I his Joey, buy me my very own wall and save my sister's B&B from financial ruin. (I was watching a lot of *Dawson's Creek* at the time.) Or maybe he'd take me to the cinema to see *Coyote Ugly* and let me eat all the bananas in his Pick 'n' Mix. That would be nice too.

In preparation for the big call, I practised my initial greeting in front of the mirror for a good hour.

'Hey there, Laurie.'

'What is up, my friend?'

'Bout ye!' (I immediately vetoed this one. Who was I kidding with the Belfast vernacular?)

In the end, I settled for a perfunctory 'Hello'. I don't recall exactly what was said. The conversation was brief, but successful. I asked the question, he replied in the affirmative and it was settled. He'd been expecting my call since Niamh's cousin, who was in his year, asked for his number.

Mel said she was proud of me for being the only one of us with the balls to ask someone they fancied to the formal. (She was taking a boy she'd kissed a few times, but wasn't particularly interested in, Nat was bringing her friend Chris along, and Niamh and Johnny were now official. Jennifer, in a different school to the rest of us, had her formal the previous year.) I was proud of myself too. It was the first time I'd done anything remotely brave. I'd never needed to. My sister and I were used to sailing through life with an emotional safety net beneath us. Our mother made it her mission to ensure nothing would hurt her girls, not the spectre of violence returning to our streets or an argument with a friend. (Mummy would invite the friend over for a playdate to eclipse all others and any bad blood was swiftly forgotten.) Much as she would have liked to drive over to Laurie's and put the fear of God into him had he turned me down, love was the one thing she couldn't control. And my mother hated not being in control.

I started thinking that maybe leaving Belfast and my family wasn't something to be afraid of after all. There was something thrilling about the great unknown, about putting yourself out there with no guarantee everything would turn out fine. I'd go on to take further leaps of faith over the years, from abandoning the security of a full-time job for the precarious world of freelance journalism, to packing up my family and moving to France for a simpler life. Plans haven't always gone the way I'd hoped. Sometimes I've fallen spectacularly on my face. But I don't regret taking these leaps. Asking Laurie to the formal was the first time I realised I didn't need a safety net.

It's easy to crave uncertainty when absolutely nothing else is going on. For once, life was quiet in our little corner of the world. Although the newly revived power-sharing executive had been suspended in February 2000 following the IRA's failure to decommission arms, devolution was restored three months later. Ulster Unionist Party leader and first minister David Trimble said he was confident the thirty-year war was over. The much-hyped millennium bug amounted to nothing, the much-hyped Millennium Dome was a flop, and everyone was playing Snake. There was something oddly prelapsarian about the summer of 2000. The following year would introduce a new normal, a reality in which shampoo bottles are carried through airport security in plastic bags, and beards and backpacks, not a Northern Irish accent, aroused suspicion and harassment. Worlds would collide once again, but for a brief while, our world had stopped spinning.

We didn't realise any of this then. The biggest story that summer was a surprise hit TV show called *Big Brother* and 'Nasty Nick' Bateman, who influenced the voting process by manipulating fellow contestants, a crime on a par with paedophilia, judging by the relentless vitriol with which the *Sun* covered the unfolding action (further vindication for my father of never buying a copy of the paper). Naturally, I was gripped. The final of the show aired on 15 September. I had to get Daddy to record it for me as this was the day of the St Dominic's formal.

Half our year left school early to get their fake tans done, waving notes from their mums claiming they had a doctor's appointment at an apoplectic Mrs Conlon. By the time my sister was entering formal season, the teachers had got wise to our deceit. Several of her class-mates, herself included, had been invited to the St Mary's formal – a boys' school on the Glen Road and Daddy's alma mater – but no one was allowed to leave early that day. So one of the girls made an anonymous call to the school secretary and said there was a bomb in the grounds. Everyone glowed orange at the formal that night.

Mummy and I went shopping for my outfit the month before the big day. I wanted to channel Liz Hurley in *that* Versace dress. Mummy told me there was no way in hell I was going out in anything held together with safety pins. She was no prude, though, and said that 'if you've flesh worth flashing' you shouldn't cover it up. I was coming out of my Isaac from Hanson phase and wanted to celebrate my newly gained femininity. We compromised on a body-con number in a brown and gold stripe with a plunging neckline and a slit up the front. More Jen Lindley than Joey Potter. I doubted Laurie would object.

Nat's mum was hosting pre-formal drinks and nibbles for everyone. It was agreed Laurie would come to the house to pick me up first. I sat my family down before his arrival with a strict set of instructions:

1. Do not offer him stew. (Nat's mum had no doubt prepared vol-au-vents and prawns in filo pastry. It's hard to compete with that level of sophistication, but the least Mummy could do was serve up a few cocktail sausages.)
2. Don't call him 'son'.
3. Don't chase the limo down the street. This last imperative was aimed at Auntie Hil, who couldn't let a seminal moment in her goddaughter's adolescence pass without incident.

I took my time getting ready in my room, the Boyzone lads looking down at me in approval as I applied glitter to my décolletage. Soon, I told myself, the posters would be replaced with photos of Laurie and me engaged in regular couples' activities, like going to Xtra-Vision on a Friday night and playfully arguing over which video to rent. He'd want *Die Hard*, I'd insist on *Pretty Woman* (another romcom that hasn't aged well), and we'd compromise and get *Scream* so he could put his arm around me during the scary bits. A shriek from downstairs interrupted my daydream. Hil. I looked out the window. Laurie had arrived.

'He's here, people,' Hil bellowed. 'Gird your loins.'

I heard the doorbell, the door opening, my mother introducing herself to Laurie and his dad. So far, so good.

'Come in, come in. Now, can I get you a bowl of stew, son?'

Cringing, I spritzed my armpits generously with Ralph Lauren Romance, took a deep breath and walked out of my room and towards my future. Laurie was at the bottom of the stairs wearing a bow tie and a look of horror. Hil had her arm around him and— wait, was she *sniffing his neck*? Even my dad let me down, shoving a VHS camcorder into our faces. Only Daddy Devlin played ball. Yes, the man couldn't speak, so had no choice but to comply, but I knew he was equally disturbed when my mother ushered me onto an arm of his chair with Laurie on the other side for a photo. He glanced at Laurie and looked over at me, shaking his head.

Our car arrived, the requisite white stretch limo. As it was too big to get up the driveway, we had to walk out onto the street. By this stage, a small crowd had gathered round to watch, including a couple of lads in Adidas button-ups, carrying hurls. One of them whistled.

'Yeo, looking good, wee girl. Who's yer man with the gay hair?'

I glanced at Laurie, a dollop of gel keeping his unruly jet-black locks in place, his bow tie endearingly askew. I was touched by the effort he'd made, though I had to acknowledge he looked out of place among the step cuts and GAA shirts.

Laurie was Catholic, though south Belfast Catholics may as well have come from a different planet. I had to save him. 'Let's go,' I said, shoving him into the limo. We said our goodbyes to my family, who appeared satisfied with the torture they'd inflicted. The limo pulled away and I breathed a sigh of relief. Then *thump*. A pair of breasts pressed against Laurie's window. Hil had thrown herself at the car. I startled. Now my cousins were banging their fists on my side of the vehicle. Coming up the rear was Auntie Bernie, five months pregnant and out of breath. I expected more from her.

'Families, eh?' I laughed nervously.

Laurie pressed the lock on the car door.

I'd love to tell you that the night was a roaring success. That I was the consummate date – flirtatious, fun, physically upright. Here's what I remember: cava in the limo; cava at Nat's; crying on Aisling's shoulder in the toilets because I thought Laurie fancied Nat; dancing to the Artful Dodger's 'Movin' Too Fast' and accusing Laurie of not moving fast enough; cava at the bar; crying on Aisling's shoulder in the toilets because I thought Nat fancied Laurie back; Aisling asking me if I wanted her to knock Laurie's ballix in; curried fried rice from Freddie's Kitchen on the way home.

The next morning, as I lay in bed stinking of fake tan and sambuca, I tried to drown out the memories, playing 'Teenage Dirtbag' on repeat, a song that felt painfully apt in the moment. I'd fought with my best friend, the boy I fancied wasn't interested, and I couldn't be sure if it was memory or hallucination, but I was haunted by an image of me standing on a table shouting 'Up the 'RA' with a classmate, whose uncle most definitely was in the 'RA. Mummy barged into the room and stood at the end of the bed, lips pursed. She marched over to the window and pulled open the curtains.

'Ah, my eyes!' I dragged the duvet over my head.

'Get up and get dressed,' she ordered. 'We're going to Long's.'

14

Revelations and a fish supper

Established in 1914, Long's fish shop, on Athol Street, is a Belfast institution. Even during the worst of the Troubles, people came from all over town to the city centre café for their fish suppers. Its windows were shattered a few times when the IRA blew up the nearby Europa – a regular occurrence. The most bombed hotel in the world was damaged by explosions thirty-three times between 1970 and 1994. Like Long's, it still stands proud today.

We had many a family celebration in Long's, birthdays and end of exams marked with malt vinegar and cartons of Five Alive. I'm grateful to be here today of all days. There's nothing like a chip butty to lift the spirits. We grab a booth and place our orders, making small talk until the food arrives. I start to relax, the promise of crispy batter easing the dread in my stomach when blindsided by another flashback from last night.

Mummy thanks the waitress and, reaching for the brown sauce, clears her throat. 'Well, girls, I have a wee bit of news for you. I'm adopted.'

I stop loading my sliced pan with chips and stare at my mother. 'What do you mean you're adopted?'

Mummy takes a sip of coffee and pulls a face before calling the waitress back over. 'Love, you wouldn't get me a wee bit more milk for that, would you?'

She turns to Toni and me. 'I mean exactly what I said. Mummy Devlin and Daddy Devlin are my parents, just not biologically speaking.'

The waitress returns with a jug of milk and Mummy smiles sweetly at her. 'Ah, God bless ya, love. May your giving hand never leave ya.'

Toni frowns. 'I think we need more information.'

My younger sister has always been the pragmatic one, waiting to assimilate all the facts before reacting. I'm glad she's taking charge of the situation, as my head has started to throb.

Mummy tells us that her mother had been married to a man named Hugh Devlin. He was from Donegal and, according to Mummy Devlin, 'a bit of a shite'. They had a son, Gogi, and after a brief spell living in a cramped room on Pilot Street, around the corner from Mummy Devlin's childhood home, they moved back into the Durham Street terrace she'd been raised in with her mother, a lodger and Mummy Devlin's older brother. When Gogi was four, Hugh was electrocuted while working as a roofer and killed. Mummy Devlin was awarded a small amount of compensation, which she wanted to use to buy a boarding house.

Her brother advised her against it. 'If you go down that road, you'll be beholden to others for the rest of your life,' he told her.

He suggested he invest the money for her in a bar, as she'd make money quickly in the licence trade and wouldn't have to work another day in her life. It was a shrewd move. My grandmother bought a bar on the Old Lodge Road, which her brother ran for her. Before long, they could afford a bigger house, though continued to live on Durham Street until their mother died.

After four years, Mummy Devlin decided to adopt. She badly wanted more children. Plus, Gogi was a handful, apparently, and in dire need of siblings. Mummy Devlin's brother thought another child would be too much for her to take on, with the bar, and by this stage they also owned a betting shop. Mummy Devlin didn't listen. She'd already started going to Nazareth Lodge, a children's home in south Belfast.

The nuns called it Open Day Sunday, when prospective parents who were registered with the home could take a child out for the day. I guess it was a bit like test driving a car. On her first visit in 1955, Mummy Devlin was led to a large, featureless room. In the corner was a playpen and, inside, half a dozen children, playing with a handful of wooden toys. Taking two paper bags of dolly mixtures out of her purse, she handed one to a girl with blonde ringlets and rolls of baby fat. Mummy Devlin said she was the double of Shirley Temple. She gave the other bag to a dark-haired toddler with a head full of cradle cap and a saturated cloth nappy. Shirley Temple took her bag of sweets to the corner of the playpen to savour alone. The second girl appraised her treasure and toddled over to the other children to share the sweets.

The following Sunday, my grandmother took the

dark-haired girl on a bus to her pub on the Old Lodge Road. It was bottling day, the one day of the week publicans shut their doors as casks of stout were delivered and decanted by hand into bottles. The floors of the pub were sticky with beer, and the smell of stale tobacco clung to the net curtains. A man with an aquiline nose stood behind the bar pouring a thick, dark liquid into a bottle, absorbed in his task. He didn't look up as they walked in, didn't acknowledge the toddler, who ran under tables, giggling, trying to get his attention. Every Sunday for a month, Mummy Devlin brought the girl into the bar to see the man, her brother.

On the last day, as they were leaving to go back to the home, the girl turned and waved at the man. 'Bye bye, Daddy.'

Mummy Devlin's brother looked up from his bottles. 'She can't go back there, Mary. Bring her home.'

He returned to his work.

After that, my mother came to live in Durham Street. She was almost two. It was Mummy Devlin's name on the adoption papers, but she was raised by both my grandmother and her brother – the man I knew as my grandfather, Daddy Devlin.

'Stop the lights.' I interrupt Mummy mid flow. 'You're telling us Mummy and Daddy Devlin were *brother and sister?*'

'It's not a big deal. Daddy never married and he wanted to help my mummy.'

'Why was he called Daddy Devlin if Devlin was Mary's married name?' Toni asks.

'He didn't want to confuse you or your sister by having a different surname to me and your aunts and uncles. So he kept his real surname for work and around his grandchildren, he's Daddy Devlin.'

I recall the time Mummy and I bumped into Gogi's friend when we were looking for a pumpkin. 'How's your uncle Jimmy doing?'

'So let me get this straight,' I say. 'Daddy Devlin is Gogi's blood uncle, but your adopted dad, not uncle, right?' My head feels like it's about to explode.

Mummy colours. 'He's my daddy, she was my mummy. They raised me together. It's very simple really. And he was more of a father to Tony than his real dad was.'

'Did people ever say anything? About them living together as brother and sister?'

'People always gossip. More about Mummy being a "widow woman", that she had all these children and no husband. But what have I told you about paying attention to what other people have to say?'

It wasn't just my mother who was adopted. The rest of her siblings were too. Hil, Bernie, Gerry, John – the lot of them. Gogi had felt like the odd one out growing up, Mummy says.

'He used to go on about not being special because he hadn't been chosen like the rest of us.'

We were full of questions now.

'Did you always know you were adopted?'

'Yes. Mummy would bring me to mass every Boxing Day, my birthday, to pray for my birth mother.'

'What do you know about your birth mother? Who was she?'

'I have no idea. And no interest in finding out either.'

'Were you born in Belfast?'

'Nope. Monaghan. I was baptised in St Macartan's Cathedral. I suppose that makes me a southerner.'

'Anything else?'

'My birth name was Marian, presumably because I was born in the Marian year★.'

And just like that, we're out of questions. *Marian.* Our mother had a different name once. Mummy has always been funny about her name, guarding it like a terrier. She likes to use her whole name when introducing herself, chin raised, as though daring someone to challenge her. She never took O'Neill when she married my father, which was quite the statement back then. And when Christmas or birthday cards arrive to the house in her married name, she refuses to open them. I know her defiance wasn't motivated by ideology. Mummy has always bristled at the word 'feminist'.

Until recently, Northern Ireland lagged dismally behind the rest of the UK when it came to women's rights. The 1967 Abortion Act wasn't extended to the region until 2019, forcing hundreds of women to travel to England each year for terminations. The near total ban included cases of rape, incest and foetal abnormality, making Northern Ireland's abortion laws among the most draconian in the world. And although women are

---

★ Running from December 1953 to December 1954, the first Marian year in the history of the Catholic Church was pronounced by Pope Pius XII. It was a year dedicated to the honour of the Blessed Virgin Mary and included special prayers and various observances.

currently at the helm of three of our biggest political parties, right up until 2017 the NI Assembly had the lowest representation of women of any legislature in Britain or Ireland.

As second-wave feminism began to take hold in the US, UK and even Ireland, during the Troubles in the North, Catholic husbands, brothers and sons were increasingly detained by the British Army, leaving it up to women to organise politically. The feminist movement in Northern Ireland, therefore, became associated with militant nationalism, the focus less on bodily and fiscal autonomy and more on civil rights concerns, like housing. While mainstream feminism took a back seat, leaving Northern Irish women behind on issues such as job discrimination, it was a psychology student from County Tyrone, Bernadette Devlin, who made feminist history, becoming, at the age of twenty-one, the youngest woman elected to Westminster until the 2015 general election.*

Until her mother died, Mummy went on civil rights marches. She was the one who encouraged us to leave Belfast, to live big and fearlessly, drilling into her daughters the necessity of insisting on equal pay for equal work. And she never expressed any great interest in our love lives. Her biggest fear was that we'd settle down too soon, before soaking up all the world has to offer. Even though she spent years cooking for her

---

* Hannah Piecuch, 'Feminism During the Troubles in Northern Ireland', *The Onyx Review: The Interdisciplinary Research Journal 2017*, Vol. 3, No. 1, pp. 37–43

brothers and father, she was, to me, a feminist. Not that she'd admit to it. I can't help thinking religion has something to do with it – Mummy Devlin's devoutness, her faith's veneration of motherhood and filial obliga-tion. You can pick and choose the elements of Catholicism that resonate all you like, but growing up with a daily dose of the stuff, it seeps into the bones and calcifies, that weight of expectation. Or perhaps embracing feminism out loud felt too much like a rejection of the men my mother loved. When you've put your father on a pedestal all your life, when his opinion is the opinion you value above all others, anything that challenges that unshakeable faith in his judgement – even if that's categorically missing the point of the women's rights movement – must seem like a betrayal.

Many years after this moment in Long's, when I realise not being kissed at a school formal isn't the worst thing that can happen to a person, I'll start to research the place where my mother spent the first two years of her life. Opened in 1900, Nazareth Lodge was the second home in south Belfast run by the Sisters of Nazareth, after Nazareth House. Collectively, the orphanages cared for more than six thousand children until their closures in 1984 and 1999. I'll read a state-ment made in 2017 by Bishop Noel Treanor, apologising for the systemic failures of the diocese of Down and Connor that led to the widespread abuse of children – including many deaths – within the homes over decades.

I'll come across the story of Margaret McGuckin, chair of Survivors and Victims of Institutional Abuse, who arrived at Nazareth House in 1960, aged three, five years after my mother left the Lodge. I'll read how, as punishment, the nuns would line the children up, pour boiling water over their scalps and cut off their hair with big black scissors. How children would cry and cry and then stop crying, knowing it was futile, that nobody would come to comfort them. How they were beaten with sticks and bunches of keys, how they were left to sit on potties for hours. How Margaret's siblings were trailed away from her and taken to Nazareth Lodge, where her brother suffered years of rape and abuse. I'll read a report that reveals some children were made to eat their own vomit and those who wet the bed were forced to put the soiled sheets on their heads. I'll read all this, and I'll get it. Why my mother wears her name with such pride. It's a name that dragged her out of the threat of darkness. That spared her the life Margaret and countless other children had. A name that meant she was chosen. A name she might never have had if it weren't for sharing a bag of dolly mixtures.

'Do you remember living in the home?' Toni asks quietly now.

'I do. And I remember the day my mummy took me home to Durham Street. It was the best thing that ever happened to me, after you two.'

'Why are you telling us all this now?' I ask her.

'I had no intention of telling you at all. It's my business and doesn't change anything. Your da made me do it.'

167

It's not the first time my father has encouraged Mummy to reveal something she'd have rather kept hidden. When I was ten, he talked her into confessing her real age. We thought she was thirty-two, but she'd just celebrated a milestone birthday. They were whispering at the cooker, Mummy stirring the porridge with ever greater vigour.

'Just tell them, what's the big deal?' Daddy said.

'Alright, alright, I'm fucking forty, is that what you want to hear? Your mother is F-O-R-T-Y!'

She started waving the porridge spurtle in the air like a woman possessed, then stormed out of the room to get ready for work. Like most things in our family, that was the last we heard of it.

The waitress comes back and puts the bill on the table. We've hardly touched our food.

'Is that everything?' I ask Mummy.

'It is for now. Oh, don't tell your cousins any of this. I don't know what their parents have told them about their situation and it's not my place to inform them. Now eat up – I want to get home in time for *Columbo.*'

15

Endings

Angela died. She was about to have a shower when an aneurysm ruptured in her brain. Hours later, my uncle arrived home. He couldn't get into the house and knew something wasn't right, so climbed in through an open window and found her lying on the bathroom floor.

Gogi called Ryan's dad, then my mum, and then a doctor. Angela was still on the floor when Mummy got there, her naked body covered in a towel. My uncle was sitting on the rim of the bath, the cigarette in his hand smoked down to the filter. He looked up at Mummy.

'She's gone, Anne.'

'Yes.'

My mother put her arms around him.

Their relationship had been strained for a while, ever since Gogi moved Angela in and my granddad came to live with us. Gogi visited once a week, chatting to Daddy Devlin about the family business while Mummy did the ironing in front of *Murder, She Wrote*. You could tell my uncle was uncomfortable. Often, after twenty minutes, he'd mumble about some urgent matter he needed to take care of at the office, squeeze the old man's arm and leave.

'He'll see that as his duty done,' Mummy would say, pressing my father's boxers with greater enthusiasm than necessary. 'That'll be him off on holiday now with a clear conscience.'

I didn't blame Gogi for feeling awkward around my grandfather. I felt the same. It was hard to know what to say to him after the stroke, how to converse without condescension. Daddy Devlin had hated small talk. He wanted to share big ideas, to challenge and be challenged. This new incarnation of the man was softer, he smiled more, watched daytime TV instead of reading. He was more like my dad's father, the sweetest man I knew. But I didn't want another Papa. I wanted Daddy Devlin back with all his sharp edges and eccentricities. I used to think he was so intelligent, he'd find a way to outsmart mortality. Turned out, his brain could get sick just like everybody else's.

My mother? She talked to Daddy Devlin like nothing had changed, like he was still the oracle on everything. It wasn't just him. She had a way with older people. When Mummy was a girl, her mother would take her on coach trips and to the bowls club with her friends. Mummy enjoyed the company of 'aul girls'. I can't remember a time when she wasn't hanging out with a pensioner, whether it was driving a neighbour to the novena, or my dad's aunt Lily to the physiotherapist (her presence came in handy the time Lily accused the man of 'interferin' with her. 'Stop your nonsense, Lily.

I've been sitting right here the whole time'), or, latterly, Moira's mum to Lidl (she assures me it's a great day out). She'd have her ladies over for slices of fruit cake and conspiratorial whispers, and they'd go home beaming. I think she made them feel seen.

My mother was thirteen when she answered a phone call from the woman living next door to the house the family owned on the Glen Road. My grandparents were out, so the neighbour told Mummy about the party the previous night and the godawful racket that had kept her awake. Mummy apologised, assured the woman she'd pass on the message, and ran upstairs to Gogi's room. Instinctively, she knew her brother was involved. Gogi was sprawled on top of the bed, the curtains in the room drawn, the smell of whiskey in the air.

'Sort it out, would ya?' he said when Mummy told him Mrs Duffy was on the warpath, turning his back to her.

Mummy put on her coat, stuffed cleaning products from the pantry into her mother's canvas shopping trolley and jumped on the number 13 bus to the Glen Road.

She poured half-empty bottles of Powers (the Catholic whiskey of choice – Prods drank Bushmills) down the sink and washed teacups filled with hash. In the bedroom, she found a small, clear balloon containing a white liquid and disposed of that too, making a mental note to ask her brother what it was. She arrived home hours later, telling her mother she'd been at confession.

Gogi didn't thank her – he didn't say anything – but the following week he took her to Jaeger and bought her a blue-lined, pure wool cape.

Mummy says not long after Angela moved in, Gogi began questioning the cost of Daddy Devlin's care, which came out of the proceeds of the family business. She told him it wasn't cheap getting help 24/7 so she could get one week's break a year, and if he wanted to move in to give her a hand he was more than welcome to.

A few months later, John told Mummy that Gogi had said she was robbing him blind over the carers. She confronted her older brother the next time he came to the house, asked him to explain himself. If he had a problem with her, then tell it to her face.

Gogi denied everything, said John was making it up. I don't think John was making it up. Equally, I couldn't imagine my favourite uncle being that callous. Sure, things had been awkward between Gogi and Mummy for a while, but something had pushed their relationship over the Rubicon. Tiny hurts and betrayals building over the years until a hairline fracture had become something unfixable.

Gogi wanted Angela buried in the family plot in Cargan, a tiny village in County Antrim where my great-grandparents came from. It was here Mummy Devlin was laid to rest twenty years previously.

At first, my mother was having none of it. Daddy Devlin was going into the grave when his time came and he certainly wasn't going to spend eternity next to *that* woman. Then she remembered something her father had told her in his more lucid days.

'If anything ever happens to me, do what causes the least ill. Don't upset the living to please the dead.'

She decided Daddy Devlin would be cremated down the line, then called the funeral directors and arranged for Angela's name to be engraved on the headstone.

Catholics tend to bury their dead within three days. Traditionally, we wake our loved ones at home the first night and in the chapel the second. (With the exception of Mummy's Auntie Annie, who had a five-day wake in her kitchen. She was afraid of being buried alive and had it written into her will that no one would even contemplate moving her before the five days were up. She hadn't anticipated dying in the middle of a heatwave. Mummy said she was leaping by the time they put her in the ground.)

Angela was my first open casket. Laid out in the good room in my uncle's house, in a black shift dress and jacket with Dynasty-style shoulder pads, she meant business, even in death.

'Doesn't she look great?' said one of the mourners, taking a chunk of egg mayo sandwich and waving it over the coffin.

'Never seen her looking better,' his friend replied. 'Here, have you seen any ham sandwiches knockin' about or is it just all that vegetarian shite?'

I peered into the coffin. It wasn't as scary as I thought it would be. I didn't agree Angela had never looked better – her permanent on-holiday tan was starting to fade – but she didn't look dead, whatever I'd imagined that to look like. She was just herself. I half expected her to sit up and tell me I was putting the pig ham back on.

The church was packed with Gogi's friends, all of Belfast society in their finery. He used to say, 'There's no society in Belfast, kid.' He hated the place. Said Northern Ireland was a hole, a dump, the same old politics, the same old shit, get out the first chance you get. The girls came for moral support, sitting in the back row, because they were hungover from an impromptu session. I did a reading in German, which seemed to make Gogi and Angela's family happy, though the language isn't exactly a crowd-pleaser and my heart-felt delivery failed to move the congregation. That job was left to Andrea Bocelli and Sarah Brightman, who had everyone in tears when 'Time to Say Goodbye' was played at the end of the service as a procession of expensive hosiery and bespoke tailoring followed the coffin up the aisle.

The priest had refused to let us play the secular song. It was a hymn or nothing.

Mummy ignored him. 'If your uncle wants "Time to Say Goodbye", he's getting "Time to Say Goodbye",' she told us, sneaking a ghetto blaster into the back of the church.

Afterwards at my uncle's house, Mummy kept herself busy, making tea and directing the caterers. She slipped back into the role she had occupied before Angela appeared on the scene – the woman of the house – ignoring the stares and the mutterings.

'Oh sure they haven't been good in years. Apparently, she robbed him blind over the uncle's care.'

Before we left, one of Angela's cousins approached Mummy and accused her of stealing from Gogi. How could she live with herself after everything her brother had done for the family and how well they looked after the old man?

Mummy smiled. 'I live with myself just fine, thanks. Cup of tea?'

That evening, she doused the worktops in Dettol, wrapped up the leftover beef bourguignon and pavlova, and helped the last of the mourners with their coats. She gave her brother a hug and left. It was the last time she set foot in the house.

Gogi still came to see Daddy Devlin, but he and my mother rarely spoke. She told Toni and me not to let the animosity between them affect our relationship with him. He'd always been good to us and we were old enough to make our own decisions. I should take him out for lunch, she said. I liked this idea. It was the grown-up thing to do. Instead of my uncle treating me, I'd be the one to look after him, for once. I booked a table at one of his favourite restaurants in town and bought myself a black blazer from Topshop for the occasion, one that said, 'I am an independent woman of means'. I asked Mummy if she could lend me fifty quid.

He looked the same – the sharp suit, the expensive watch – and acted the way he'd always acted, making phone calls and smoking throughout the meal. He never asked his dining companions if they minded him lighting up while they were eating. I heard Mummy tell Auntie Bernie once it was because he was a selfish bastard. He talked about Angela the whole time, laughing and telling jokes. And then he'd stop laughing and telling jokes, and he'd sit there and stare at the tablecloth as though it has all the answers. And I thought Michael Stipe was spot on when he said everybody hurts (I was cultivating an appreciation for alternative rock at the time). Everybody *does* hurt – even selfish bastards.

Mummy was knitting a Royal Mail post box when I got home. 'Did you have a nice time?' she asked.

'Yes. He seemed really sad, though.'

'Did he now? Shit. I've just dropped a stitch.'

The rift between my mother and uncle had a ripple effect. Gerry and Bernie rallied round Mummy, while Hil refused to take sides. True to form, John didn't have much to say on the matter. He was married to Liz (Auntie Roseleen dug out the holy water when she heard) and living in England, away from the drama. I wondered whether it was inevitable, the breakdown of my mother's family. Since she told us about her adoption the previous year, every time I saw her with one of her siblings, I'd see further differences between them. People used to say how alike my mother and her sisters were, but on closer inspection, all they had in common was the same dark hair and the childhood memories.

Of course, that's the important stuff, the shared history, though I didn't appreciate that then. I was fixated on blood, and kept quizzing Mummy on her birth mother. Did she know anything about her? What if she had siblings out there? Real ones? Didn't she want to meet them? Mummy told me to give her head peace. She was 'no fuckin Jessica Fletcher' and had zero intention of hunting down her biological family. Ever.

Four months later, I was in the school library with Mel, studying for our English Lit. mock A level. It was a drizzly November morning. I hadn't seen much of Gogi since I took him out for lunch, though I heard from Nat, whose dad mixed in vaguely similar circles, that he'd moved a woman called Penny and her daughter into the house. Mel and I were discussing Sylvia Plath and how she killed herself aged thirty. Mel said she sympathised with Plath as thirty is 'really fucking old', when Mrs Mulvenna, the librarian, came up to us and told me I had a call in the secretary's office.

It was my dad. 'It's Daddy Devlin, love.'

Mummy and Auntie Hil had been in Boston on holiday a day when Daddy Devlin had his second stroke. They got the next flight home and drove straight to the hospital. Daddy Devlin was lying in the bed, his eyes closed. He looked restful, like he was contemplating his next chess move.

Mummy walked over to him and began fixing the pillows behind his head.

'Right, Daddy, what's all this about? My first holiday in a year and you go and create a fuss over nothing.'

For the next six days, it was the same routine. She arrived first thing with a flask of coffee and sat knitting by his bedside or reading *Woman's Own*. She rubbed fresh pineapple over Daddy Devlin's cracked lips. She'd been down this road before with her mother and knew what was coming.

'I'm afraid that won't be possible,' the consultant told her, when she asked him to discharge my grandfather. 'We don't have an ambulance for you, for one thing.'

'Well, I'll hire my own ambulance then, doctor. I'll do it with or without your help, but I'm taking my father home to die.'

Daddy Devlin came home on 12 December. Mummy had set up a hospital bed for him in the front room, the window to his left overlooking my grandmother's rose bush. For the next four days, my aunts and uncles came and went, keeping a vigil by their father's bedside. They swapped stories of misdemeanours from their childhood, Auntie Hil's cackle filling the house. Gogi was there, a temporary ceasefire between him and Mummy putting us all at ease. Daddy made ham sandwiches and chicken soup, going back and forth to the bakery for Belfast baps, mainly for Auntie Bernie, who Mummy said was like an 'eatin house detective'. She was seven months pregnant with our Caoimhín, her fourth child. Mummy and Hil said she looked like the Michelin Man and Bernie gave them the finger and called them hateful fuckers. It was like old times.

That Saturday, I had tickets to take my younger cousins to the Steps concert. I didn't want to leave Mummy, but she encouraged us to go. I think she wanted a bit of quiet in the house. She knew it was time. They were all there around the bed when Daddy Devlin slipped away in my mother's arms. A robin appeared on the windowsill. The garden bird was a favourite of Daddy Devlin's, one of the first to start the dawn chorus and the last to stop singing at night.

'Let's wash Daddy,' said my mother.

The funeral was a private affair in the house. Just us and Father Joe, who said all our family masses until he came out and had to leave the priesthood. That morning, I came downstairs just after dawn and found Mummy in the living room. She'd lit a turf fire – Daddy Devlin had always loved the smell – and was sitting in an armchair beside the coffin, drinking a mug of tea. The robin was back at the window.

'That's Daddy Devlin, you know,' she said, not turning around. 'He's come back to us as a robin.'

As far as I was aware, Catholics don't do reincarnation. Even in death, my grandfather wasn't going to play by the rules.

16

2001: A sex odyssey?

My parents started house-hunting the following spring. The area had been going downhill for a while, car-jackings and theft the crime of choice in Andersonstown. You'd have been mad to leave anything precious in the car. When Daddy stopped at Curley's after visiting the crematorium to collect my grand-father, he had to bring Daddy Devlin in with him, the urn placed on the kids' seat of the trolley as he did the shopping for dinner. There were further acts of antisocial behaviour. After our local was burned down, a superpub sprang up in its place. Every evening, without fail, punters used our driveway as a urinal as they staggered home.

Our homeless friend Podge had long vacated the hedge out the back. In his place, glue-sniffing teenagers arrived. Daddy came across one taking his bike 'for a wee dander' around the garden. He told my father that God had sent him to save us.

'That's great, son, but where do you live? Let me get you home.'

The boy was too far gone to converse, and after a few minutes cycled off unsteadily down the path.

'This place has gone to the dogs,' Daddy said to Mummy later. 'We need to move.'

Since the IRA ceasefire, this had become our new way of life. Without the paramilitaries around to put the fear of God into Andytown's feral youth, lawlessness and disorder reigned. The firmly binary choice – vigilante kneecappings or having your car stolen – didn't appeal to my parents, and with Daddy Devlin gone and me going to university in the autumn, the Manse was too big for my family now.

I was off to Trinity College (the one in Dublin, not Cambridge, though TCD alumni like to say it's the Oxbridge of Ireland). We visited the university on a day trip to Dublin when I was seven and apparently, standing outside the front gate of the old campus, peering through to a large cobblestoned square filled with students carrying books, I told Mummy I'd be going there when I was older. I'd say it was more Dublin than the academia that appealed. We'd taken a horse and carriage ride around St Stephen's Green that day and Mummy bought me and Danielle matching silver Claddagh rings as a symbol of our enduring friendship. Mine had an emerald in the middle, Danielle's a ruby. Who knew, just three years later, it would be a ruby that would tear us apart – the ruby slippers she wore as she took her bow in front of an adoring audience in *The Wizard of Oz*.

Later, when it was time to start looking at universities, I couldn't help but be impressed by Trinity's alumni. All the Irish creative greats went there – Beckett, Wilde, de Burgh. (Though Mummy was none too pleased with the 'Lady in Red' singer when she found out he'd been sleeping with his children's nanny. It's a shame we have to skip 'A Spaceman Came Travelling' on the Christmas compilation album.)

Though the last British Army watchtower was dismantled in 2006, ending the visible border between north and south, we'd been able to travel freely to Dublin since the mid-nineties. That wasn't always the case. The time I went with Danielle we were stopped at military and customs checkpoints along the way and eyed suspiciously by soldiers, who knew they were a target for republican military groups. Now you can zip down the M1 to the capital in two hours flat. It's funny to think that from Northern Ireland you need to take a flight to get to other parts of the UK.

I wasn't going to Dublin alone. Mel and Nat would be there. Mel had enrolled to study drama at Trinity, and Nat, an arts degree at University College Dublin (UCD). In it for the long haul with their Protestants, Niamh and Jennifer had decided to stay in Belfast, Jennifer already in her first year of Law at Queen's University. (Her frequent rows with her line manager at Debenhams over incendiary devices in the cookware department had stoked her appetite for debate.) We spent our last few months together driving around the Lisburn Road in Nat's silver Honda Civic, high on Quavers and Chicane's 'Saltwater'.

I was ready for the next stage at last. I had it all planned out, college life. I'd drink black coffee in beatnik cafés (I read an article that said the Kerouac crowd were back in vogue), learn to play the guitar, spend my Erasmus year in Rome, and fall in love – requited this time. I hadn't seen or heard from Laurie since the night of the St Dominic's formal, and Ryan was at university in Newcastle (the one in England, not the seaside town in County Down, where Catholics like to holiday). But it was okay. I'd made peace with the lack of romance in my life. School wasn't my time, I told myself. University, now that would be the moment I'd figure it all out, when I'd discover my true calling and meet the man I was meant to be with – a deep thinker, who also played the guitar. Maybe we could start a folk duo?

I didn't need to meet him right away. It was important to spend time getting to know the new – or real, rather – me. I was a woman about to embark on an intellectual, creative and sexual odyssey. It was a good year for female self-discovery. Everyone was at it – Christina Aguilera unleashing her inner burlesque dancer in 'Lady Marmalade', Britney's electric 'Slave 4 U' performance at the VMAs in bejewelled pants, a Burmese python around her neck. It was time. Time for our awakening.

'Are you planning on getting a degree in the midst of this awakening?' Daddy said from behind the *Daily Mirror*.

'Stop listening in on our conversation!' I sighed theatrically, and turned back to my sister, ignoring her attempts to concentrate on her GCSE mock double chemistry paper – a year before the actual exam. 'Ugh, he's being so annoying.'

My father couldn't understand why I had to leave home to study. Queen's was a perfectly good university, he told me at least twice a day.

'And just what kind of job are you going to get with a BA in Germanic languages?'

Said the man who went to art college. I'd figure it out. Employment wasn't the sole purpose of higher education. I needed to grow.

'Grow up, more like,' he scoffed.

'Ignore your father,' said Mummy. 'He doesn't get it.'

She got it – why I needed to move away. She wanted a bigger life for me too. Though it wasn't easy for her to let go. In less than a year, she'd lost a parent, was leaving the area she'd lived in her entire life, and her first-born was about to fly the nest. After twenty-two years of cooking in industrial-sized pots, the only people she had left to look after were my dad and sister. Daddy was working all the time and Toni had never really needed looking after. My mother was in uncharted waters. Of course, true to form, she shared none of this with us and focused her attentions on house-hunting.

We were heading up the Falls on our way back from town a few weeks before I was due to leave, the replacement for our most recently stolen lawnmower in the boot. As we sat in traffic in front of the Bobby Sands mural, me singing along to 'Drops of Jupiter' – *She checks out Mozart while she does Tae Bo, reminds me that there's a-room to grow, hey hey, yeah* (Note to self: take up Tae Bo at Trinity. Sexy musician types seem to dig it) – Mummy announced she had something important to discuss and turned off the radio.

'Hey, I was listening to that.'

'If you're going to be having sex when you're at university, you must use protection.'

'What?' As predictably unpredictable as my mother was, the abruptness of her ambushes never failed to throw me.

'Condoms, the pill, whatever it takes. You know I'm no fan of putting unnatural substances into your body, but rather the pill than having a baby at this juncture. Though, if you do have a baby, I'll look after it until you finish your studies.'

I needed a moment to digest. This was a woman who couldn't entertain a conversation about periods.

'Okaaay. Where has all this come from?'

'My goal was to get you to eighteen with a good education and beautiful teeth. And I've achieved that. You're on your own now. What you do with your body and your life is up to you, not me or your father. He might have different ideas, but don't listen to him. All I'm saying is, if you end up with fillings and want to have sex with everyone around you, that's your business. Just be safe about it.'

'But—'

'Look. I can tell you not to do these things and you're going to do them anyway and feel like you can't tell me anything. This way, maybe you keep me in the loop from time to time.'

Ah. I looked across at my mother. She was staring straight ahead, hands fixed firmly on the steering wheel. I wanted to reach over and give her a hug, but I knew better.

'Sure, Mummy. I'll make an appointment with Dr McAuley about the pill tomorrow.'

She nodded and turned the radio back on.

After months of searching, my parents had made an offer on a house. As soon as Daddy laid eyes on the Edwardian double-fronted semi on a quiet street lined with cherry and apple blossom trees, it was a done deal. It was more than the blossom. This would be the first place of their own, Daddy's and my mother's, free from any association with his in-laws. The Glen Road house and the Manse had belonged to Daddy Devlin before us, and much as my dad respected and, I think, loved his father-in-law, he was relieved to move on, out of the shadow of the older man and the never-ending drama of his wife's family.

There was nothing Mummy didn't consult Daddy Devlin on. Daddy used to say she couldn't evacuate her bowels without running it by him. She didn't care. In her eyes, my grandfather was the I Ching, a man beyond comparison and reproach. I'd never heard her say a bad word about him – or my grandmother. This bothered me, mainly because it exposed my own short-comings as a daughter. Mummy had nursed two dying parents and gave up her job to be there for her family. In the build-up to leaving home that summer, I couldn't be there for my family for the duration of a meal. I'd inhale dinner, then run up to my room, playing Alanis Morissette on repeat while I got ready to go out. (I couldn't very well go off to university listening to the Backstreet Boys, and as I never got into Alanis during

her *Jagged Little Pill* days, I suspected her retro appeal
– six years on – and feminist agenda would go down
well with my new peers.)

I was heading to Nat's one evening and running
uncharacteristically late trying to decide if a 'Hands off
my melons' top was too much for a night in in front
of *Buffy the Vampire Slayer*. With Nat's sleepovers, there
was always the possibility we'd end up going out, so I
stuffed the top into my backpack just in case and threw
on a denim jacket with a sheepskin trim. My taxi
waiting outside, I pushed on Mummy's bedroom door.
She'd gone to bed that afternoon after finding out a
friend from her Federation days had died suddenly. I
was surprised by her reaction. Mummy didn't take to
her bed. Even after Daddy Devlin died.

She was lying in the dark under the covers, her back
to the door. Daddy was in London for work and Toni
away on a school trip.

'Mummy?'

'Is that you away, love?' She didn't turn around, but
I could tell by her voice she'd been crying.

'Yeah, my taxi's here . . . Are you okay?'

'I'm great. Just a little tired. Say hi to the girls for
me.'

I started fiddling with the zip on my backpack. 'I
could . . . stay in if you like?' Even I wasn't convinced
by the offer.

'Why would you do that? Everything's fine. I'm fine.
Go out and have fun. I'll be fine.'

Three fines. 'Well, if you're sure, then?'

I walked over to the bed and kissed the back of her

head. 'I won't be late. Maybe we could do something tomorrow? Go for a run out to Bangor, get some fish and chips?'

'Sounds good, love. Don't keep your taxi waiting.'

I didn't. And not even Angel telling Buffy she was the one freaky thing in his freaky world that made any sense to him made me feel like anything less than the worst daughter in the world that night.

My parents hadn't planned on moving to east Belfast. No one from our area would have dreamt of crossing the invisible divide. You may as well have moved to east Berlin. When Moira found out they'd settled on a property near Stormont – 'the seat of unionist oppression, Anne!' – she didn't speak to Mummy for a month and said not to expect her to visit. I laughed when Mummy told me. Moira had always been a bit of a Chucky,* but then so were most of the girls at my school. Her reaction seemed excessive, though.

What I didn't know then was that Moira's father had been arrested and held in Long Kesh camp as part of Operation Demetrius, a policy of internment without trial, introduced by Stormont's unionist government and approved by British Home Secretary Reginald Maudling. On 9 August 1971, the Army arrested more than 340 Catholics, many of whom had no connection to the IRA. During the operation, paratroopers opened fire, killing ten people, in what became known as the Ballymurphy massacre, later dubbed 'Belfast's Bloody

---

* The English-language pronunciation of *tiocfaidh*, slang for an IRA supporter, not the demonic, serial-killing doll.

Sunday'. The victims included a priest tending to a man who had been shot, and a mother of eight. One of the homes raided that morning was Moira's. On discovery of a first aid kit, soldiers dragged her father Eoin, a construction worker, out of the house, claiming he was a medical officer for the IRA. He was released after a number of weeks without charge.

Almost exactly four years later, on 1 August 1975, Eoin's seventy-eight-year-old father was travelling home from a bingo night in Banbridge with a group of fellow pensioners when gunmen opened fire on their minibus. He was shot in the head and died instantly, along with the driver. At the time, it was widely believed the UVF were responsible for the attack, which came two days after the murder of three members of the popular Irish cabaret group the Miami Showband by a gang of UVF and UDA members. A few years ago, it was revealed that the guns used in the shooting were linked to the IRA, who, in seeking revenge for the Miami Showband massacre, mistakenly targeted the minibus instead of a police van. The IRA continue to deny any involvement in the killings.

My parents and sister moved in to their new home in November 2001. The following day, Moira turned up on the doorstep with four coconut fingers and a box of teabags.

In early September, two months before the big move, loyalists in the mainly Catholic area around the Holy Cross primary school in Ardoyne began picketing the entrance to the school, in response to attacks on

Protestant homes. As parents walked their children, aged between four and eleven, to the Catholic primary school on the interface between the two communities, the protestors hurled insults – and then stones, bottles, fireworks and even a pipe bomb – during the weeks of unrest. Each night, on the news, we'd see children in tears, gripping their parents' hands as they were led along a road lined with riot police and soldiers.

'God almighty, I don't know what's wrong with this place,' Mummy said.

For once, it wasn't just Northern Ireland making headlines. Days later, I was standing in the kitchen of the Manse trying to work out how to cook an omelette – Daddy said I couldn't very well live off vodka and Bird's Eye potato waffles for the next four years, and Nat said that was exactly what she was intending on doing. I wasn't paying much attention to the news in the background. I'd managed to burn the arse out of Daddy's new frying pan and knew I was in for it when he got home from work. I turned to scrape my failed egg into the bin under the sink, when out of the corner of my eye I saw a plane crash into the World Trade Center. I ran to the bottom of the stairs and shouted up at my mother, who was sorting through Mummy Devlin's boxes in the attic. I don't know how long we stood there together in front of the TV, silent as we watched the world change before our eyes. Six weeks later, the IRA announced it was giving up its guns.

Before I knew it, it was time to leave. Niamh came around that morning with a box of university essentials she'd put together – stationery, chocolate, and a mug for all the coffee-drinking I was planning on doing. I'd said goodbye to my classmates at the party Mummy threw for us at the end of term, after our leavers' mass, where Father Thomas said he'd never seen so many orange faces. Everyone went back to mine to change out of our uniforms (at last we could rejoice in our autonomy!) and into low-rise camel-coloured trousers (you wouldn't have been seen dead in anything else), joining our parents and our drama teacher Mrs Watson downstairs for a cold buffet and slices of buttercream cake. As we made our way to the pub, arm in arm, someone requested the Ryan song and I obliged.

Aisling called me a 'rocket', before imploring me to 'never fuckin' change, ya wee weirdo'.

The car was packed, Daddy impatient to hit the road. 'Calm yer knickers, Micky! Just one more photo.' My mother ordered Toni and me to stand outside the front door, where she'd forced us to stand at the start of every school year for a decade. Toni handed me a good luck card she'd made with photos from our childhood. I hugged my sister and hopped in the back seat. 'Good luck on your sexual odyssey!' she called after the car as we pulled out of the driveway.

A few weeks later, Mummy and Auntie Bernie sealed the last of the boxes, Caoimhín crawling between their feet, his babble bouncing off the bare walls.

Daddy called. He was leaving the office soon and would bring tea in with him. Did they fancy a Chinese from that posh place beside the new house? They did those crispy duck pancakes with the sliced cucumber.

Sure, sounds good. Mummy hung up the phone.

Bernie and Caoimhín had gone on ahead to the house. There was no one left. Mummy stood in the doorway of the empty front room and remembered. That's where she sat when she was 'stepping out' with my dad, on a brown paisley-print sofa, listening to The Beatles. (She would have preferred Des O'Connor – it was a painful education, Daddy said.) That's where Toni took her first steps. That's where Daddy Devlin lay in her arms as she told him it was okay to let go.

A cough behind her. The removals man was hovering at the door.

'Is that everything, love? The traffic's mad now, so it is. You'd want to be getting on the road.'

Mummy nodded, picked her mother's rose bush up off the floor and left, without looking back.

'That's everything.'

PART TWO:

THEM

1

The outsider

There's a legend that's been doing the rounds at Trinity for years. Apparently, if you're Protestant, on a certain day of the year you can climb the university's Campanile – the 100-foot-tall granite and stone bell tower built in 1853 by Belfast architect Sir Charles Lanyon – in Front Square, and shoot dead a Catholic with impunity. Oh, and if you pass beneath the Campanile's bell as it tolls, you'll promptly fail your exams.

All academic institutions have their urban myths and I'm reasonably confident no Catholic has ever been taken out by a Protestant from the Campanile. The prejudice was real enough, though. Trinity College Dublin was founded by royal charter in 1592 on land appropriated from an outlawed Catholic priory. (That's why you'll flunk your exams if you walk underneath the ringing bell tower – the monks are said to have cursed it in revenge.) The university refused to admit Catholics for 200 years, at which point the ban was lifted, with various restrictions. In turn, up until 1970 the Catholic Church in Ireland told its followers not to set foot on campus, attendance constituting a 'moral danger' to the faith.

Fifty years on, you'll find all faiths and none at Trinity, yet its reputation as a bastion of Protestant elitism endures. UCD, where Nat went on to study after we left St Dominic's, typically attracts a Catholic majority, from wealthy Dublin suburbs and rural areas across Ireland, whereas Trinity tends to be more popular with international students, old-money Irish and anglophiles. (When I was at uni, a 'West Brit' referred to someone who was born in Ireland but felt more connected to the culture and history of the UK. Now the insult has expanded to include everything from preferring Walkers crisps to Tayto, to the unironic appreciation of red corduroy trousers.)

Nat, Mel and I embraced the (mostly) good-natured rivalry between our new stomping grounds. Mel called us stuck up; we marvelled at the sartorial boldness of her fellow south County Dublin classmates – O'Neill tracksuit bottoms and a Ralph Lauren polo shirt (in a different colour every day of the week). They say a Trinity degree gives you an advantage on the international stage. But a Trinity student would be hard pushed to get a job in Dublin because no one could be arsed listening to them.

I didn't care about the stigma. Every day for five years (it was meant to be four – we'll get to that) as I passed through the ancient oak main gate, beneath the archway leading to the front square, I had to pinch myself. *I get to study here.* To the left of the quadrangle is the chapel, to the right the exam hall, grand neoclassical buildings that flank the Campanile, surrounded by maple trees. Michaelmas term, when the leaves glow red and gold, was my favourite time of year, the smell of endless possibilities in the air. (FYI: endless possibilities smelt like old books and new stationery.)

Behind Front Square you'll find the arts block, a brutalist, concrete structure, generally regarded by Trinity's arts student populace as a carbuncle on the otherwise flawless complexion that is their hallowed campus.★ Most of my lectures took place here and most of my socialising on the Ramp, the disability entrance to the building. If you wanted a cigarette in between classes, to meet up with friends before heading to the pub, to see who was around, and to be seen, you hit up the Ramp. The vibe was humanities chic – think moth-eaten cashmere, and bicycles with baskets. At the far end of campus, the science and engineering lot – also known as Those Who *Do* Have A Fuck's Notion What They Want To Do With Their Lives – congregated around the Hamilton building, where the vibe was I'm Not A Pretentious Arsehole (i.e. GAA jerseys and bikes without baskets).

The Ramp was especially popular with privately educated students from the UK, collectively referred to as Team England. It was easy to spot a member of

---

★ The arts block was built in the 1970s as a practical solution to the boom in the student population, thanks to the introduction of free higher-level education, more women going to university and the church lifting its Trinity ban. So, you know, it wasn't all bad.

this tribe. The guys wore woven bracelets, made for them by children whose homes they helped build during the volunteering stint of their gap years, and keffiyehs, to show their solidarity with the Palestinian cause. We showed our support for the Palestinian cause in west Belfast, but if you started walking down the Falls in the traditional Arab headdress, you'd be advised to get your head checked. Floppy hair was in (boys); brushes out (girls). Team England hosted suppers, where they served culinary curiosities (for a girl whose first encounter with an avocado was in her thirties) such as chicory and venison, slain by the host on a straightforward shooting weekend. (It was at one of these dinner parties I proclaimed the prized game the best bit of beef I'd ever tasted.) They holidayed at the family villa in Ibiza (the bohemian part of the island, not San Antonio, where Niamh and Mel spent a lost week the summer before we started uni), and at the end of a long day consisting of two arduous thirty-minute tutorials enjoyed a vermouth and tonic at home – similar aromatics to G&T, but less alcohol.

That's not to say this crowd didn't drink to excess. Their hedonism made our Crescent nights out look like WI meetings. A guy in my linguistics class turned up to a lecture one Monday morning in the same clothes he'd been wearing the previous weekend. He told me he'd just come from the airport. That Friday night, he and some friends played the drinking game Dice Man, inspired by the eponymous cult novel by Luke Rhinehart. Every decision rested on the dice. Roll a six, you had to get a taxi to the airport; a three, you were on the next flight out of Dublin. He spent the weekend holed up in a five-star hotel room in Prague with two Australian backpackers. (The dice made him do it.)

I was fascinated by this group when I first arrived at Trinity. Fresh from their gap years, they seemed so self-assured. I'd floated the idea of a year abroad before starting university. It would be an excellent opportunity to find myself, I told my parents, but Mummy said the only thing I'd find if I brought it up again was her toe up my hole. Like every other arts student on the planet, my privately educated peers had yet to figure out their calling in life, but they knew with unwavering certainty that everything would be fine. Better than fine. Throwaway declarations made after a couple of pints – 'When I'm running Goldman Sachs . . .' – became self-fulfilling prophecies. Oddly, I saw nothing boastful in these assertions. It made perfect sense that Team England would go on to achieve greatness – they'd never been presented with an alternative. Actually, that's not entirely true. They could choose to fail, to opt out of life's myriad responsibilities. But when these guys checked out, they did it in style.

One of the most striking things about my new classmates was their ability to argue. They ventured opinions freely, without fear of judgement. Conversations segued from the Iraq war to threesomes, and no topic was off-limits, including politics. It took me a long time to get comfortable with this kind of candour. You never discussed politics back home unless you were among friends.

I was invited to a Team England dinner during my second year at Trinity. After our lamb tagine, plates were cleared to make room for a mint Viennetta. I was ecstatic. It was a Tuesday night – what had prompted such spoiling?

Our host Jen apologised. 'I'd no time to make a proper pud, guys, so we're eating retro tonight.'

Everyone chuckled and Joff, the guy sitting next to Jen, said the eighties had called and wanted its dessert back. I didn't get it. *Is Viennetta not the height of culinary sophistication?* (I'm not joking. There was a time I genuinely thought Viennetta was the height of culinary sophistication.) Jen poured coffee into colourful vintage tea glasses she'd picked up in one of the souks on her last visit to Marrakech and I forced myself to take sips. My coffee-drinking plans hadn't panned out. I didn't enjoy the bitter taste, but everyone else drank the stuff, so I persisted. It was starting to dawn on me that self-discovery wasn't the key to being socially successful at university. Tribalism was. And that was something I knew all too well.

The conversation turned to Northern Ireland. Or rather, Joff interrupted a breakaway chat I was having with the boy next to me – about a guy in his boarding school who once ate twenty-two bowls of porridge in one sitting – by bellowing, 'Guys, what should we do about the Northern Irish problem? Personally, I think we should give it back' across the table.

Give it back. Like you'd return a Tupperware dish after devouring its contents.

'I think it's a bit more complicated than that,' I said,

unsure where I was headed. Politics, debating – this was new territory for me. For the first time in years, I could feel my palms starting to sweat.

'Oh ya, you're from Northern Ireland, right?' Holly, a doe-eyed philosophy major, sitting opposite me, reached for a piece of Fairtrade dark chocolate in the middle of the table. 'What do you think we should do?'

I didn't know how to respond. I thought it was strange that Joff and Holly should consider the reunification of Ireland a decision for the English alone, not a consultation with Northern Ireland – more than half of its citizens would have, at that stage, preferred to kneecap themselves than lose their British identity – or with the Republic, for whom unity would have serious economic repercussions. (Northern Ireland gets around £10 billion a year in British subsidies. Funding this gap would put a severe strain on Dublin's finances.)

I could have said that. I *should* have said that. But that was all I had. Those Irish history books my father had given me years previously remained unread. The truth is, I'd spent so much time obsessing over boys and boozing and, latterly, getting out of Belfast, I wasn't interested in learning about my country's past. We need to move on, I'd tell my parents whenever they tried to educate me about the Easter Rising or the War of Independence, whenever they wanted to share what life was like during the worst of the Troubles. Still, thanks to Miss Rooney, who frequently ranted about the wounds inflicted on the Irish by 'them Brits', I knew enough to be irked by the ignorance of the people sitting at the table around me. They hadn't a clue about the country they were living in, a country whose fate they shaped. Worse, they didn't care.

Before I could answer, Holly followed up with, 'Are you a Catholic or a Protestant?' It was a simple question and yet one I'd rarely encountered. She didn't do the dance we did at home, the sussing out which side of the divide someone's from by asking what school they went to. 'I'm Catholic,' I stuttered. 'Actually, it's funny, no one has ever really asked me—' She'd already moved on, scolding Joff for throwing a piece of chocolate at her head to get her attention.

It was the first time I'd spoken about home in a political context with an outsider. And it surprised me, my English peers' indifference, the chasm in their knowledge concerning the shared history of our islands. But what right did I have to be annoyed when I barely knew anything about where I came from myself? Besides, I didn't want to be a craic killer. We already had a reputation for being difficult, us Northern Irish. So I buried whatever flicker of annoyance had begun to stir in me, and when Jen asked me if I'd like more coffee, I handed her my cup.

2

Way harsh, Tai

I'm getting ahead of myself. Let's rewind to those first few months at university, to a time before tagine and the Joffs of this world. I lived with a family in Dundrum, a suburb of Dublin, miles from campus and, fun fact: home to Ireland's largest shopping centre. Had I planned things better (i.e. focused on the practicalities of leaving home instead of planning my sexual awakening) I would have applied for a place in the halls of residence months earlier, like Mel had. Nat had offered me a room at hers. Her parents owned a house – a smaller version of their home in Belfast with the same plush, neutral décor – which she was sharing with her sister and two other students.

I was tempted. At school, Nat's house had been my second home and, given the horror stories surrounding student accommodation, the prospect of a functioning heating system, never mind the added luxury of a radiator cover, appealed. But Nat lived near UCD's campus, a thirty-minute bus ride from Trinity, and my prospective housemates were all UCD students. I had no problem with this, but I needed to be where the action was, within a stone's throw of one of those beatnik coffee shops where I'd meet the future love of my life. So I turned Nat down, left it too late to get into halls, and a week before moving to Dublin found myself with nowhere to live. Naturally, my mother (who had taken a back seat that summer because I told her I was eighteen and could take care of my own accommodation) was at hand, ready to remedy the situation. She knew a woman, whose sister had a friend in Dublin who took in student lodgers. Seven days later, I moved into Mrs O'Brien's.

The night my parents dropped me off, Mummy surveyed my new bedroom and nodded in approval. Just off the kitchen, it was small, but warm and clean, and even had an en suite. (Mummy never cared much for en suites. She didn't know why anyone would want to sleep next to where they conduct their business. Keen, however, to maintain an upbeat tone and delay the inevitable moment my father burst into tears as we said goodbye, she could talk about nothing else. 'Ooh Alix, look – you have an electric shower and everything!')

The bed had already been made up, but Mummy swapped it for the new linens we'd bought together, then helped me unpack my books. I put Niamh's mug on the desk in the corner of the room along with a family snap taken at Disney World in Florida. It was one of my favourites, even though I was deep into my bumbag phase at the time. With nothing left to do, Mummy said it was time to get on the road. Right on cue, Daddy started to well up.

'Jesus, Micky, keep it together,' Mummy said, pulling me in for a hug.

'You've got this, girl,' she whispered in my ear, leaving me to console my father while she went to thank Mrs O'Brien for the tea and biscuits.

I heard the car reverse on the gravel driveway outside, and they were gone. I was on my own for the first time in eighteen years. I expected to feel sad or apprehensive, but I couldn't wait to get stuck in to college life. Tomorrow, I'd get the bus into town to check out the campus. Maybe meet Mel for lunch and a couple of Jägerbombs to celebrate the start of our new adventure.

The next morning, I walked into the kitchen to the smell of warm soda bread and a table set with brightly patterned crockery. Mrs O'Brien, a petite woman with an assortment of floral aprons she wore on daily rotation, remains the only person I've ever met, with the exception of my parents' next-door neighbours, who set the table for breakfast the night before. (At first, Mummy thought this was a Protestant habit. I explained to her it's simply a habit of someone who has their act together.)

Breakfast soon became the highlight of my day. It wasn't just the homemade marmalade and eggs boiled to order that I loved. Sitting around the table with Mrs O'Brien and my fellow lodgers felt like home. There was Steffi, from Switzerland, who had come to Ireland to 'learn English, drink Guinness and meet cute musician guys who like to play their fiddles', and from Japan, Nao, whose only word of English was 'yes', which was confusing as she was never up for doing anything.

'Do you want to go to the cinema, Nao?'

'Yes.' (Remains seated.)

Not that Mummy made her own preserves or soda bread. And the one apron she owned she set fire to, making hot milk for Weetabix. But she was always there, sitting across the table in the mornings. And that was something.

Occasionally, we were joined by Mrs O'Brien's daughter. Although she was in her mid-twenties, she didn't seem to have a job to go to. Like Mummy, she was fond of her dressing gown and often wore it to dinner. She never spoke to us, which was understandable. Her mother had been taking in lodgers for twenty years – I'm sure she was sick of the sight of us. Most days, she'd pick at her plate in silence, others she'd snap at Mrs O'Brien and storm off to her room. Sometimes, she'd start crying, literally over spilt milk, and Mrs O'Brien would pretend not to notice and ask if anyone wanted an extra rasher. Steffi reckoned she was depressed. I'd heard of depression, though my understanding of the complexities of mental illness was limited. After Daddy Devlin died, Mummy didn't lie in bed all day or cry that much. She got up, saw us off to school, watched her detective shows. I assumed she was fine, too caught up in teenage angst to notice the grief in her eyes.

I didn't see Mel until the Freshers' Fair later that week as she was busy settling into halls. Front Square was lined with stalls promoting Trinity's numerous clubs and societies. It was an important business, deciding

which to join. Was I a Grand Epicurean Order girl?
(The former incarnation of the Food and Drink Society.
You can see why UCD hated us.) Or a Player? (Trinity's
drama soc., not a club for smooth operators. I wouldn't
have got a foot through the door.) I'd just signed up
to the latter when I heard a familiar voice.

'Lix! Man, over here!'

It was Mel. Carrying a pile of books and wearing
jeans and a pale blue polo-neck, she looked great,
collegiate. She introduced me to Chloe and Anna,
friends from halls. Chloe was English and taking the
same course as Mel, Anna from the Bahamas. The only
thing I knew about the Bahamas was that it was where
Moira went on holiday a few times. She could go to
the West Indies, but not east Belfast.

'Are you joining Players?' Mel asked, slipping her
arm through mine as we walked to the next stand. 'It's
meant to be great fun.' She sounded different. More
anglicised.

The four of us walked around for a bit, evaluating
societies according to the number of free drinks they
were prepared to offer upon membership. Based on
this important criteria, I gave Amnesty a miss and joined
the surf club. Mel and Chloe had to rush off to a
lecture. Mel gave me a hug and said we'd see each
other soon. I watched her and Chloe as they walked
off, and felt the same pang of paranoia I experienced
when Mel first started hanging out with Nat. I could
try to befriend Chloe and Anna to prevent being edged
out of Mel's life, but I didn't think tailing them back
to halls or suggesting we go for a scooter ride down

to the poke shop was the right approach this time. Making friends at university would be a whole different ball game and I was starting to realise I didn't have the playbook.

Apart from an introductory lecture welcoming the latest intake of Germanic Languages students (that's German, Swedish and Dutch; and no, I haven't a clue what I was thinking either), I'd no classes scheduled for the rest of the day, so took myself off to see *American Pie II*. I'd considered *Amelie*, which was showing at the same time and would have been a more sophisticated choice in keeping with my new scholarly existence. But in times of uncertainty, there's nothing like familiar comforts, and what I needed right then was popcorn with a side of scatological humour. En route to the bus stop after the film, I took a detour to St Teresa's, a church just off Grafton Street, Dublin's commercial hub. Every time I visited the city as a child, Mummy would pop in to light a candle for a special intention. I loved the solitude of the place, sitting in the pew at the back of the chapel, surrounded by the warm glow of a hundred flames of hope.

It was pouring down when I left. I sprinted to the corner shop at the top of Grafton Street and bought two packets of Tayto crisps and a Snack bar, then hopped on the number 14 back to Dundrum. I popped my headphones on as the bus pulled away. There was only one CD in my bag. I'd been playing Kylie's *Light Years* on repeat for a month. When the album had dropped the previous year, the diminutive singer was hailed the comeback queen, resplendent in gold hot pants. This was her moment, the media cried. She'd been written off at the grand old age of thirty-two, but Kylie had proven her critics wrong. Maybe I didn't need to figure everything out at university. Maybe my thirties would be my time.

The further we got from town, the less sure I was I'd ever figure anything out. What if I'd made a mistake leaving Belfast? It had been less than a week and already I missed my family. The O'Briens and Nao were having lasagne when I got back. It made me think of Niamh, whose speciality was the layered pasta. I told Mrs O'Brien I wasn't hungry and went straight to my room, had a shower and got into bed with my Tayto crisps and a *Sex and the City* boxset. I'd forgotten about the episode where Carrie compares dating to the Troubles: *As I sifted through the rubble of my marriage skirmish, I had a thought. Maybe the fight between marrieds and singles is like the war in Northern Ireland. We're all basically the same, but somehow we wound up on different sides.* This reflection seemed less profound on second viewing, and I also had a thought. Maybe Carrie was a bit of a dick? I was about to skip to the next episode when my phone went. It was home.

'Well? Are you having a good time? How's it all going there?'

I hadn't the heart to tell her. 'Never better, Mummy.'

A week later, determined to step up the efforts to make new friends, I auditioned for the Freshers' Co-op, a glorified panto, which ran for six nights midway through Michaelmas term, and was written, directed and

performed by Trinity students. I felt reasonably confident my A level in theatre studies would secure me a
place among the fifty-strong cast members (roughly
the same number of students worked behind the scenes),
and prepared Nina's monologue from *The Seagull*. The
audition took place in a sparsely furnished room in
front of the play's four directors – third-year students
and Co-op alumni. There was no need for my monologue, one of the directors – a guy with a polo-neck
and thick-rimmed black glasses – said, before inviting
me to stand in a circle of fellow auditionees for a round
of Zip, Zap, Boing, an 'energy-building ice-breaker'.
There wasn't much to the game – a lot of pointing at
your neighbour and yelling 'zip' or 'zap'. If you were
feeling daring, you boinged someone. Evidently, my
boing lacked conviction, and I didn't make the cut.

I wasn't entirely friendless that first year. My course
mates were lovely people, but it was about six weeks
before any of us dared to suggest a drink after class.
Mainly, I hung out with Steffi or stayed over at Nat's.

One night, we were watching a reality TV programme
about models. The prize was a contract with a top
London agency.

'Isn't that Yer Man Jamie?' said Nat, pointing at the
screen.

A skinny guy with excellent bone structure was
strutting down a makeshift catwalk in a hotel conference
room in a pair of orange briefs. It was Ryan's friend
from the ill-fated ski trip years earlier.

'That's a bit of a Calvin Klein look going on there,'
cooed one of the judges.

'Wow, he's growing into his looks, isn't he?' I said. 'Still not a patch on Ryan, but fair play to him for putting himself out there. He might get the odd modelling job out of it.'

Mel and I saw each other a handful of times that first term. She had me over to halls for drinks with her roommates, and we'd meet for the odd lunch in between lectures. It was hard to pin her down, though, and we just . . . drifted. I told myself she was too busy with her new friends to bother about her old ones, when in reality, I was jealous. Of the way Mel made friends so easily, of her ability to fit wherever she went. 'Mel's changed,' I told Nat, outraged at the audacity of the betrayal. Of course, we change all the time, and the friends who stick are the ones who realise that, who accept that the constants in our lives are not always constant. Who don't hold us to the films we loved at fourteen or the crucial world views we held at seventeen – 'But you're obsessed with Nick Carter. Now you're saying Kevin is the hottest Backstreet Boy?? Who *are* you?!'

I let my resentment build, creating an awkwardness between us that culminated in a drunken argument when we were home from Dublin with Nat one weekend. Niamh, Jennifer and Sammy joined us at my parents' house for a Cresurrection, an ode to our teenage days. I dug out my pleather halterneck and Puffa jacket, and Sammy dusted off his white jeans and set up strobe lights in the kitchen. None of us can remember what started the fight, which involved Mel and I tossing butter and coffee granules at one another in an ineffectual manner and, later, me stomping into my bedroom, where Mel was spooning Nat, and Nat a pound of Golden Cow after she decided she needed to wax her stomach hair and that Niamh, as the sensible one, should be the person to do it.

I'd changed into a crocheted Aztec-print bikini. 'Check it out, Mel – I bought the same Next bikini as you, but it looks better on me because I can *tan*.'

On the scale of friendship low blows, it was right up there with Tai telling Cher Horowitz she was a virgin who can't drive, and clearly not my finest hour. We laughed about it the next day and moved on, but it was years before that awkwardness fully evaporated. All because I felt too embarrassed to tell my friend I was lonely.

3

You're not Coolio

'I'm not going back next year,' I announced, as my mother pulled into Belfast Central station. It was a Sunday evening in November and I was nearing the end of my first term at Trinity. Most weekends, I took the train up home to watch *Pop Idol* with my parents.

Mummy sighed. 'Give it till the end of first year. If you're still not happy, you can come home and go to Queen's, but you have to give Dublin a chance. I bet you'll be having a ball by Christmas.'

'Whatever,' I said, giving her a reluctant kiss on the cheek and climbing out of the car. 'See you next weekend.'

I didn't see her the following weekend. I met Dan at a traffic light ball organised by the students' union a few days later. The dress code was red if you were in a relationship or not interested, amber if persuadable and green for all systems go. I wore a lime top covered in emerald sequins and an olive eyeshadow. Mel introduced us. A schoolfriend of a guy she was in halls with, Dan was a Londoner with a cheeky grin and broad tastes. Studying Classics and Italian, he was as much into Socrates as he was soccer. I immediately imagined introducing him to people back home – an *English* boyfriend. Who spoke *Italian*. Dan and I snogged that night, though not in the middle of the dancefloor like I used to do with Laurie. University relationships are a classier business. We shifted on the stairwell instead.

We talked too. About everything and nothing. I went back to his flat that night and stayed there for two days, in a freezing box room that smelt of damp. I didn't mind because I had found him. The One. When I eventually resurfaced, Dublin was in technicolour. I went to St Teresa's and lit a candle – thank you, Our Lady! You have sent him to me!

Dan and I didn't see each other over the Christmas holidays. I resisted the urge to invite him up to Belfast to meet my parents as it had only been three weeks and Nat told me that was definitely too soon. (I waited until the week we got back to college.) Before term ended, I'd decided to move closer to campus. Steffi had returned to Switzerland and Mrs O'Brien's daughter went from crying over her cornflakes to staring murderously at me over her toast. It was time to move on. I found a room in the large basement flat of a Georgian terrace off O'Connell Street. My flatmates were third-years – Miles, a bona fide member of Team England, who liked to have sex with his girlfriend in my room-mate's bed, once while I was there (by the time I'd plucked up the courage to announce my presence, it would have been creepy to interject, so I stayed under the covers); Alice, my roommate, who, fortunately for Miles, was never there; and Cillian, half-Greek, half-Northern Irish: he embraced this duality by downing cans and smashing plates in the living room. We hit it off as soon as I told him my dad had directed 'Fred, there's no bread'.

'I mean, there's nathin' worse than running out of a sliced pan, y'know?' said Cillian. 'Imagine being hungover and having fuck all in the house for a wee bacon sandwich. Doesn't bear thinkin' bout.'

On Valentine's Day, Dan presented me with a purple rose he bought from a street vendor at 1 a.m. on a trip to Budapest with his classmates and carried all the way back to Dublin. He made me steak and chips, and for dessert melted a Mars bar in the microwave, serving it on top of a block of vanilla ice cream from the Centra on the corner of his road. Then we danced to Linkin Park. I was convinced romance didn't get much better.

So when Dan ended it over pints and chips in the Buttery, one of the on-campus bars, a fortnight later, I was stunned. He was very sweet, very considerate, told me I was great, it just wasn't working.

'But . . . no one has ever melted a Mars for me before.' I sobbed fat, salty tears on his shoulder for half an hour.

When I eventually pulled myself together, giving Dan a farewell hug (holding on slightly longer than appropriate), I ran across Front Square, out onto College Green and into the phone box overlooking Trinity's main entrance in all its splendour. The battery had died on my phone and I urgently needed to speak to my dad, the Yoda of lonely hearts.

'Ah, love. I know the pain,' he sympathised, as I cried down the phone. 'It reminds me of the time your mother went on holiday with her friends when we were eighteen. A Turkish waiter took a shine to her and gave her some perfume. And she wore it when she got back. Can you believe it? Hurts like it was yesterday.'

I'd heard about Mummy's 'betrayal' numerous times and couldn't quite make the connection between that and Dan dumping me. But it felt good to hear Daddy's voice at the end of the line, and in that moment I missed Belfast more than ever.

Undefeated, I made one last-ditch attempt to win Dan back. The Trinity Ball was coming up, the biggest social event in the university calendar, where you had the privilege of paying seventy quid to wear black tie, listen to bands you'd never heard of, and queue for an hour at the bar in Arctic conditions while losing all your friends. It was the pre-ball house parties that really mattered, and if you were lucky enough to get an invitation to one, you were almost guaranteed to have a good night, so well-oiled by the time you got to the main event, you weren't bothered by the queues or the cold.

I got zero invitations.

'Why don't you host your own party?' Mummy suggested when I was home the month before the ball.

'I don't think anyone would come.'

'They'd come if they didn't have to pay for their own drink.'

The following weekend, my parents drove down to Dublin, bottles of vodka, gin and wine, and crates of beer clinking in the boot of the car. It was a crude attempt to buy me a social life and I loved them for it. I invited everyone I knew to the party, including Dan (it felt like the grown-up move, friendship with the ex), Nat, Mel and her friends from halls and Team GL (my Germanic Languages course mates – that's what we called ourselves). Mel and Nat couldn't make it, but I was confident the evening would be a success regardless.

The day of the ball, I got up early and made a play-list of the classics – Haddaway, Hanson (obviously), Len's 'Steal My Sunshine', 'Gangsta's Paradise' for some urban flava.

'Don't say "urban flava" again,' Toni urged, when she called to wish me luck. 'You're not Coolio. And don't do the rap either. Just be normal.'

I got my hair and make-up done in the afternoon and calmed the nerves with a vodka and orange juice while I got ready. My dress was laid out on the bed – a black, knee-length number, with a modest slit up one leg, the opposite to my Liz Hurley dress. *Tonight, Matthew, I'm going to be classy, demure, sober.*

Before the guests were due to arrive, I filled clean ashtrays with crisps as we'd run out of bowls, and chucked a throw over the sofa – it looked like Miles and his girlfriend had paid it a visit. There was nothing left to do but wait. I hit play on my iPod – *Here comes the hot stepper, murderer* – poured myself another vodka orange and toasted the air. 'Here's to a night to remember.'

Seven people turned up. Team GL – I knew those guys wouldn't let me down – and Hannah from Team GL's roommates. My playlist, however, was a hit, and people really seemed to appreciate the premium own-brand crisps I'd splashed out on. As I'd been warned, it was downhill from there. I didn't bring a coat with me, hoping Dan and I would reunite and he'd wrap his tux jacket around my shoulders like they did in the movies. As I stood on the cobblestones outside the Buttery, watching Dan kiss a girl from his class, tucking a loose strand of hair behind her ear, I finally got the literal meaning of giving someone the cold shoulder.

I had an insight (bear with me). Maybe boys were overrated and romance wasn't the point of the university experience. You might meet someone and it lasts or you might meet someone and it doesn't last or you might not meet anyone at all. And that wouldn't be the worst thing in the world. (That's as far as I got. I suspected there was more to discover about life and love, but my head had started to spin and my feet were throbbing. It was time to go home.)

Cillian was sitting on the street outside the flat when I got back, his bow tie undone, drinking from a bottle of beer. The night sky was full of stars, the scent of fresh vomit in the air.

'Hey, girl. Good night?'

I puffed out my cheeks and sat down beside him, pulling off my heels.

'It gets easier, you know.'

He handed me his bottle and I took a swig. 'I feckin hope so, dude.'

I hit the reset button that summer, remembering some-thing Mummy told me Daddy Devlin had said to her when I was four. A place had come up last minute at St Catherine's, but Mummy thought it was too soon for me to start school – I'd be the youngest in the class, which would surely put me at a disadvantage.

'Take the place,' her father advised. 'She'll need that extra year down the line.'

He was right. I wasn't prepared for my first year at Trinity. For one thing, I faced up to the reality that I wasn't cut out for a triptych of languages, especially one I'd spent seven years trying to ditch. So I changed courses the following September – to Italian and Classical Civilisation (yes, that was Dan's degree. What can I say? He made ancient history sexy) – and re-entered first year with a renewed sense of optimism.

I moved in with Nat and auditioned again for the Co-op. My 'boing' perfected, I landed a small part in the show. Mummy and Daddy drove down from Belfast to see me on opening night and got clamped after parking in the city centre.

'Ah, but it was worth it to see your eldest daughter tread the boards, right?' I asked Mummy.

'Are you kidding me?' she laughed. 'Worst play I've ever seen.'

On the first day of my second-time-round first term, I met someone. Ruth was sitting two rows in front of me in 'An Introduction to Homer' wearing a pair of bright green boots and shaking a head of closely cropped curls in indignation as she argued with the guy next to her about the need for a female translation of *The Odyssey*. She knew stuff – about books and politics. (But not drinking. That was one area in which I was her sensei.) She was the only girl in her year to wear a tux to her school formal and one of the few people I'd met at Trinity who didn't pester me to say 'I'll blow you up' in my 'scariest Gerry Adams accent' when drunk. We didn't click immediately. Ruth was horrified I'd been at university a year and was unable to locate the library, and couldn't understand why anyone would wear a miniskirt without tights in November. I found her prickly and private at first, with more friendship red lines than my mother. She also shared my mother's mafioso-like loyalty, and the more I hung out with Ruth, the less I missed home.

There was another someone. A boy who hailed from south of the border. We met at the Co-op after-party, and after a year of friendship started dating. But his isn't my story to tell, and besides, this isn't *that* kind of love story, so let's just call him Mr G. All you need to know about him is that he had an unironic appreciation for red corduroy trousers and is one of life's good ones. Like Mel, he had that social ease that helped him fit into any crowd, and came with a readymade group of friends from school and Trinity, who I liked immediately.

I was an exotic addition to Mr G's closest circle, a confident bunch, for whom diversity was someone who didn't go to boarding school. They were full of opinions about the North, namely that we were troubled and troublesome, the Beirut of the West. It bothered me.

'You have to understand,' Mr G tried to explain. 'Every time Northern Ireland was on the news, you guys were throwing stones and petrol bombs at each other and wearing balaclavas. It was terrifying.'

Mr G had a friend, Ed, whose dad was from Newry, a town an hour's drive from Belfast, close to the border and a hotspot during the Troubles. He moved to London in his twenties and became a successful corporate lawyer. Anytime he needed to push through a difficult deal, he'd revert to his Northern Irish accent in an attempt to intimidate the opposition. It always did the trick.

Before leaving home, I never considered myself an angry person. Loud, emotional, dramatic, sure. Yet whenever I engaged in what I considered to be a friendly debate down the pub with Mr G's friends, I'd be told to 'Calm down', 'Relax', 'You're a mad woman'. *The Mad Woman of Andytown.* Debating wasn't something we did much of as a family, mainly because we couldn't. (And my mother was a champion debater at school.) An impassioned point of view was invariably taken as a personal attack, so we avoided controversial topics. A couple of years ago, Toni and I got into a heated discussion over whether or not the Kardashians were feminist role models, and didn't speak to each other for two days.

I used to marvel at how Mr G's family weren't afraid to get stuck in to meaty political discussions whenever they got together. The youngest of six, he and his siblings had been encouraged to debate around the dinner table from the moment they could talk. Everyone fought their corner, but there were no tears, no storming out of the room. I think, maybe when you've grown up surrounded by the language of conflict and division, it bleeds into your psyche, your world view, your inter-actions with others.

When I started going out with Mr G, his friend Tom said he didn't consider me Irish. It stung, and seemed like an odd thing to say for a guy who went to boarding school in the UK and had an English mother.

'Of course, I'm Irish,' I fumed. *Watch yourself, don't get angry.*

'No, you're Northern Irish. It's different.'

It was true. I didn't grow up watching the same shows as Tom and Mr G, didn't share their cultural references. Even Tayto crisps tasted different up north. We were from the same island, but to Tom, my Irishness was not the same as his Irishness. There was only one other person from the North in our group. Georgie's parents were Irish nobility and she spoke with an upper-class English accent, as many Anglo-Irish do. Georgie remains a good friend and the best of people, but I don't think she'd disagree when I say she was, to many of our peers at university, the acceptable face of Northern Irishness. I was a wild card, a curiosity, my Falls Road upbringing and the way I pronounced my 'ow' vowel sounds giving me an edginess I certainly didn't possess at school. I didn't dwell on this, because for the first time since I left home, I didn't feel alone.

4

The greening of the east

I graduated from Trinity with a Desmond, a 2:2, the drinker's degree, indicative of neither greatness, nor great dissoluteness like my Team England counterparts. I was reassuringly average. To celebrate this achievement, I went on a three-month backpacking stint around Australia and Thailand, meeting up with Nat and Niamh, who had spent the year travelling around the world. After eight weeks, I ran out of money and returned to Belfast with a nose piercing and a pair of fisherman's pants I refused to take off for a month.

I had every intention of vacating my parents' house – the following year, when the plan was to move to London to study journalism. I'd whittled my future career choices down to war correspondent – my background gave me the hands-on experience employers love – or editor of *Vogue*, mainly so I could use the line, 'Florals? For spring? Ground-breaking'. (*The Devil Wears Prada* was released that year.)

'And what do you intend on doing until then?' my mother demanded as I sat in my fisherman's pants watching Fern and Phillip on *This Morning* corpse over the word 'Uranus'. 'If you're going to live here, there'll be no more lying around in front of the TV. You need to find a job.'

The following day, she marched me into a recruitment agency in town, which, as luck would have it, had an opening for an administrative assistant. Officially, my role was to stamp timesheets and file documents. Unofficially, I poked friends on Facebook and revelled in the linguistic challenge of updating my status. (I refused to participate in the widespread acts of grammatical vandalism committed on the addictive new social networking site – 'Gráinne is: wants a chip butty'.)

Being back home was easier than I thought it would be. Change was in the air in 2007. By the end of the year, Belfast would host Ireland's first gay arts festival and open its first Ikea, enticing busloads of shoppers from as far as Cork across the border. I know what you're thinking – who wouldn't travel 260 miles for a Swedish meatball? But when I was growing up, no one in their right mind would have dreamt of venturing north for a daytrip. It was too dangerous. More exciting than flatpack furniture and the death of the three-piece suite was the DUP's historic power-sharing agreement with Sinn Féin.

That May, Ian Paisley, a man who once denounced the pope as the antichrist, and Martin McGuinness, a former IRA commander, became Northern Ireland's first minister and deputy first minister respectively. Imagine Batman and Joker, Cartman and Kyle, Taylor and Kanye sitting side by side to lead their country into a better future. These former arch-nemeses not only made it work, they became close friends, the press calling them the 'Chuckle Brothers' because they cracked so many jokes together. The partnership lasted just over a year, at which point Paisley resigned, as members of his party didn't approve of the bonhomie he shared with his deputy. He died in 2014, McGuinness three years later.

I grew up with Ian Paisley. He was the gay-bashing firebrand on our TV screens every night, the man who said Catholics 'breed like rabbits and multiply like vermin'. To Protestants, McGuinness was beyond redemption, a remorseless murderer. But during their short-lived partnership, they brought a brief period of stability to Northern Ireland and a civility to our politics. There was a sense we could shape our own future – Paisley once said to McGuinness, 'We don't need Englishmen to rule us; we can do that ourselves' – and as my mother said, 'put all the dickery behind us'.

It almost went tits-up before it started when, a few months before the new assembly met for the first time, loyalist Michael Stone stormed the entrance hall of Stormont armed modestly with a knife, a handgun and a bomb, yelling, 'No Surrender!' before being wrestled to the ground by security. The ex-UDA member rose to infamy after killing three mourners at a Provisional IRA funeral at Milltown Cemetery in 1988 and confessed to shooting dead three Catholics between 1984 and '87. (Before his failed attack at Stormont, his biography, *Stone Cold*, was serialised in the *Sunday Life*. My father was hired by an ad agency he did regular work for to make a commercial promoting the publication. Stone's voice dried up during filming, so the agency director went to get him a glass of water.

'I'm not touching that,' Stone said to Daddy. 'I bet yer man's knobbed it.'

'What do you mean?' asked Daddy.

'Stuck his dick in the glass! Nah, man, not going near it.'

To prove the water had not been knobbed, Daddy had to take a sip.)

Life was a little quieter on the home front. I wasn't going out much – only Niamh was around. Mel had moved to London and had landed a job in TV, and Nat and Jennifer were living in Dublin. I travelled down most weekends to see Mr G. It was the height of the Celtic Tiger, Ireland's economic boom, a time when a thirty-euro main course was considered reasonable, champagne standard on a night out, and everyone drove an SUV. Once a month, Mr G came up to Belfast, satisfied his kneecaps would remain intact for the duration of his stay. The first time I brought him home when we were at university, the colour drained from his face as we pulled up at a set of traffic lights beside a mural of two masked gunmen alongside the words, *We seek nothing but the elementary right planted in every man – the right if you are attacked to defend yourself.*

My parents had settled in well to life in east Belfast. Before they moved, they visited the local church in their new neighbourhood. Daddy wanted to make sure the area was safe for Catholics.

A fifteen-minute drive from the house they wanted

to buy, beyond the coffee shops and pizza restaurants, Union Jacks hung from every lamppost and wooden pallets and tyres were stacked 40 feet high, in preparation for the Twelfth bonfires. I didn't know any Protestants living in Andytown, but I imagined the 'Prods out' spray-painted across the wall outside the leisure centre wouldn't have been the best welcome to the neighbourhood.

The parish priest assured them there'd never been any trouble. They were in middle-class suburbia now. In time, other Catholic families would follow. Mummy and Daddy called the west Belfast exodus the 'greening of the east'.

It took them a while to get used to the peace and quiet. Their first month in the house, Mummy saw two policemen walking down the street without army protection. Forgetting she no longer lived on the Falls, she ran outside in her bare feet and was about to shout at the men to get inside to safety when she realised. *No one is going to hurt them here.*

A few weeks later, a man in a dog collar rang the doorbell. Without giving him time to speak, Mummy dragged him inside.

'Ach Father, come in, won't ya? Do you want a cup of tea? So good of you to welcome us to the area. Here, you wouldn't do a wee blessing of the house while you're here? Come in, come in out of the cold!'

Toni informs me our mother literally dragged the man by his sleeve into the kitchen and started rooting around in a drawer for a bottle of holy water. Thrusting it into his hand, she knelt in front of him, pulling Toni down with her, and bowed her head, ready to receive his blessing.

The man cleared his throat, seizing his opportunity to get a word in.

'My dear, I'm not a priest. I'm a minister from the local Presbyterian church. I wanted to speak to your neighbour, but she's not in, and I thought you might know where she is. I'll bless you anyway. It's all the same God, after all.'

They enjoyed the company of their Protestant neighbours, Ian and Joan, and Joan's parents, Ivan and May, who lived next door. One day, May was listening to Radio Ulster. Tom Hartley, a Sinn Féin councillor and former lord mayor of Belfast, who ran tours of the City Cemetery, had written a book about the graveyard's history and was telling the presenter he'd love to be buried there, but stood no chance – the waiting list was huge. May happened to have a plot spare. Her parents had bought her one, but she wanted to be buried with Ivan. She got Tom's number off the radio station and said he was welcome to it, free of charge. (Tom was our old neighbour, back when we lived on the Glen Road. Mummy would give his ex-wife Joelle milk from the goats and she used it to make cheese.) As a thank you to May, Tom arranged a private tour of the cemetery for her family and their neighbours, which included my parents, and everyone was surprised to learn of an underground wall, built to separate Catholic and Protestant graves. Like I said, sectarianism runs deep in Northern Ireland.

5

Say nothing

Just when life seems to be settling into some kind of vague normality, Mummy does it again. Another bomb-shell dropped without warning. We're in the queue to pay at the local petrol station, reminiscing about the time Uncle John caught Toni stealing a chip off his plate and went nuclear.

'Ah sure, like father, like son,' Mummy says, rooting through her bag for her wallet. 'Gogi was exactly the same.'

'Huh?' I said.

'Your uncle John. Takes after his da.'

'Daddy Devlin?'

Toni, always a step ahead, places a steadying hand on my arm. 'Wait. Are you saying Gogi is John's *daddy*?'

Mummy shushed her. 'Stop telling my business to everyone in the shop.'

'You just told your business to everyone in the shop! I can't believe you—'

Toni's silenced by The Look, a glare of such burning intensity, its recipient bursts into flames on the spot.

(Okay, not quite, but when Mummy dishes out The Look, you know better than to argue.)

'Who's next?' We've reached the top of the queue.

Mummy asks the woman behind the till for a lotto ticket and hands over a copy of *Hello!*. Wayne and Coleen Rooney are on the cover, beaming in front of a giant twenty-first birthday cake featuring a decorative pair of pink Louboutins, a Chloe handbag and some Chanel sunglasses.

'Ach, isn't she gorgeous? I just love her,' says the cashier.

'Lovely girl,' Mummy replies. 'So down to earth.'

By the time we get home, our mother is ready to talk. She makes herself a cup of coffee and the three of us sit down at the kitchen table. She tells us Gogi was twenty-one when he had a one-night stand with Laura, who was in her last year at St Dominic's. When she told our uncle she was pregnant, he said he wanted nothing to do with the baby. Laura left school without taking her exams and moved to a mother and baby home in London, where she gave birth to a boy, John.

My grandparents knew nothing about Laura or the baby until Mummy Devlin found a letter Laura had sent to Gogi not long after she gave birth. A visitor arrived a few weeks later. Mummy Devlin answered the door to a girl with long, straight hair and heavily kohled eyelids. She shook my grandmother's hand and was led into the front room. They sat down, the three of them – Mummy Devlin, Laura and my mother – a tray set with Minton china (Mummy Devlin rarely brought out the Minton) and a plate of Rich Tea biscuits on the table between them. Mummy remembers only fragments of that first meeting. Laura's bare legs – she'd never seen a hemline that short. Her mother apologising – my grandmother never apologised. 'I'm sorry you had to go through this alone. I know my son is no good.'

John had already been placed with a couple in England, who were planning on adopting him. Mummy Devlin convinced Laura to let her raise the baby. If she went through with the adoption, she'd never see John again. But if she gave him to my grandmother, she could see him whenever she liked, and when the time was right, he'd know who his real mother was.

That evening, Mummy stayed in her room as instructed, her ear pressed against the door.

'If he comes to live with us, I'm leaving,' Gogi raged downstairs.

'Don't let me stop you.' Mummy Devlin. Calm. Determined.

The front door slammed. Mummy creeped out onto the landing and peered over the banister.

'It's not our concern, Anne.' Her father was standing in his doorway, unshaven, his eyelids heavy.

'Sorry, Daddy.' She returned to her room.

Gogi didn't leave, though he made himself scarce when Laura arrived the following month with the baby, barely three months old.

'This is your new brother,' Mummy Devlin told her children.

Gerry and Hil looked inside the crib. Gerry shrugged. 'He doesn't do much. Can I call on Davey now?'

I knew Laura. She used to come to the house to visit Mummy once or twice a year when she was in town. A senior executive for a big ad agency in London, she travelled the world with her job. The first time I saw her, Mummy gave her a hug and grabbed her hand, Laura's bangles jingling as Mummy introduced her as an old friend of her mother's. I'd never met anyone like her. She smelt of cloves and sandalwood, and always brought a present for Toni and me – perfume or a silk scarf picked up on one of her trips abroad. I had no idea she was from Belfast originally. She spoke the Queen's English in posh, husky tones.

Laura is John's mum. This information alone was hard enough to get my head around, never mind the additional revelation about my uncles. Gogi and John weren't brothers – they were father and son. How could I not have seen it? They had the same scowl and, although you couldn't make out what John was saying half the time, the same appreciation for the multifarious nature of the word 'fuck'. Despite these mind-blowing similarities in their characters, I can't say I ever witnessed any particular bond between the two men. Gogi appeared to treat John in the same way he treated Uncle Gerry – with a tolerance occasionally bordering on contempt.

I couldn't stop thinking about my grandmother. How it must have felt to discover the existence of her grandchild in a letter she wasn't meant to see. Tony was her only biological child. John was her blood, he was Daddy Devlin's blood, his grand-nephew. That mattered. Didn't it? Nature, nurture. Since Mummy told us she and her younger siblings were adopted, I kept returning to the age-old debate. Are we the inescapable product of our genes or the embodiments of our environment? My grandmother had said her son was no good and Mummy often told us she felt special being adopted. Was my uncle, as my mother put it, 'a selfish bastard' because that was his essential character? Or was his character shaped by circumstance – losing his father at a young age and being the only child of five not 'chosen'?

I hadn't seen Gogi since his wedding to Penny the previous summer. We weren't expecting to be invited. It had been two years since we last saw him at my twenty-first birthday party. He and Mummy had barely spoken more than two words to one another in the intervening years.

The invitation to the wedding came late in the day – Hil and John had received the nod weeks before. Like us, Bernie and Gerry were last-minute additions to the guest list. Mummy and Toni said they'd no interest in going, but my father felt turning up might help salvage our relationship with Gogi, opening the path for reconciliation between brother and sister. (Daddy fancied himself the peacekeeper of the family.)

Our taxi pulled up outside the church. Gogi was greeting guests in a black tuxedo, looking devilishly handsome as always. A little greyer, perhaps – he was in his sixties at this stage. I wondered how he'd react when he saw us. How his friends would react. Most of them I'd known all my life.

I took a deep breath and looked across at Daddy. 'You ready?'

'I could do with a couple of jars, but aye.'

I needn't have worried. Gogi welled up when he saw us.

'Hey kiddo. You came.'

His friends smiled and asked after Mummy and Toni. When it was time to leave, I hugged Gogi goodbye and suggested we go for lunch sometime. He said he'd love that and to give him a call. We both knew I never would.

That was it, I thought. A rather poetic ending to a family saga that involved discovering your mother, aunts and uncles bar one are adopted, your grandfather is your uncle's uncle, and your grandparents are siblings. To top it all off, there was a German in the family plot. I certainly wasn't expecting to find out that my uncles were not, in fact, brothers, but father and son.

Mummy's itching to get stuck into *Hello!* but we're not letting her off that easily. 'Did John always know that Laura and Gogi were his biological parents?' I ask.

'No. He found out later.'

'How late?'

'I don't know. He was twenty-four or twenty-five, I think.'

'When he discovered he was *adopted*?' Toni is incredulous.

'He always knew he was adopted,' Mummy says, curtly. 'He just didn't have all the details.'

Jesus, the woman can be hard work sometimes.

'Well, can we have all the details please?' I say. 'You brought it up, after all.'

She tells us. How she was walking down the stairs with a basket of laundry one morning when a voice called from above. 'Anne?'

She looked up.

John was hanging over the banister at the top of the house. 'Can you get me a copy of my birth certificate? I need to renew my passport.'

'No problem, son. I'll have a look for it in a bit.'

Fuuuuuuck she mouthed as she went to put a wash on.

Later that afternoon, when her father was up (Daddy Devlin kept unusual hours. He often stayed up all night reading and went to bed at 8 a.m. His body clock was the perfect foil for his reclusiveness. Being asleep half the day meant you weren't around to receive visitors), Mummy cornered him on his way into the kitchen. He'd been in the garden doing his Canadian Air Force routine, an eleven-minute workout comprised of five exercises, designed in the 1950s to bring fitness to the masses.

'John is looking for his birth certificate. What do I do?'

Daddy Devlin walked over to the stove and warmed his teapot over the gas hob. He sunk a spoon into a tin of loose-leaf Darjeeling and added it to the pot, then opened the cupboard above the cooker.

'Have you seen the honey? I could have sworn I put it back in here last night.'

'Daddy. Are you listening to what I'm saying? What should I tell John?'

'Ah, there you are!' He reached into the back of the cupboard and pulled out a jar of acacia and a packet of oatcakes, placing two onto a plate. He took a banana from the fruit bowl, so ripe its innards had started to burst through the brown skin, got the milk from the fridge and poured just a dash into his cup with a spoonful of honey. When the tea was ready, he tipped it over his milk and honey using a strainer. He walked over to the kitchen table, sat down on his chair and bent his head, a moment of quiet gratitude for what he was about to eat. My mother recognised this daily ritual, one of many small, everyday acts my grandfather imbued with meaning. She sighed and waited for her father to finish. He took a bite of his oatcake and, satisfied he'd masticated for the appropriate amount of time, turned to Mummy.

'Leave it. It's between John and Tony.'

'That's it? Leave it? John will go buck mcnoon when he finds out!'

'I'm serious, Anne. Don't get involved. It's not our place.'

Of all Mummy Devlin's sayings, the one our mother employed the most was 'Keep your own council'. The worst thing you could do was broadcast your business to the world, and the second worst thing was broadcasting someone else's business.

There's a Seamus Heaney poem called 'Whatever You Say, Say Nothing', in which he describes Northern Ireland as a place 'where tongues lie coiled' and the people as 'cabin'd and confined', communicating through 'whispering Morse'. Secrecy was ingrained in our psyche in the North. I grew up in a culture of avoidance. When something was too sensitive or painful to discuss, it wasn't discussed. We said nothing.

Mummy gave John his birth certificate a few days later and, as predicted, he went 'buck mcnoon', though not initially. Laura's name was on the document, but not Gogi's. John told Mummy he'd always suspected Laura was his mother. She paid particular attention to him when she came to visit and people used to comment on how alike they looked. He asked Mummy if she knew who his father was.

'I can't tell you that, son. You'll have to ask Laura.'

'Well? Did he ask Laura?' Toni leans across the table, chin resting on palm, hanging on our mother's every word.

'He did.'

'What did he say?'

'What do you think? He went toke. "Why didn't you fucking tell me? Fuck this fuckin' mad family", bla bla bla. That's when he left home.'

I remember John moving away when I was about ten. I knew he went to France for a while. He also spent time in England, getting to know Laura better, Mummy tells us now. After a few years he came home and moved back in with Daddy Devlin and Gogi.

'Did he have it out with Gogi? And did Gogi ever apologise for what happened?' I ask.

'I have no idea,' says Mummy. 'You'll have to ask him that yourself. Though Gogi paid for John to go to flying school when he came back.'

John had stopped working for the family business, and when he returned to England he got a job as a pilot for an air ambulance.

'Did the others know? Hil, Bernie, Gerry?'

'No. When John told them, Hil was furious. She demanded to know what I knew about her background.'

'Do you know anything?'

'Of course not. Right, we're all done here. I want to read my magazine in peace.'

That was the end of the discussion. Mummy had installed an invisible electric fence around the subject. As far as she was concerned, my sister and I required no further information. Recently, sensing a softening in her stance, I asked her if she felt guilty for not telling John sooner.

She hesitated before answering. 'No, because if I accepted responsibility for that, then I'd have to accept responsibility for everything, for all of their issues. And I'm not prepared to go there.'

They fuck you up, your mum and dad, isn't that how the poem goes?★ It wasn't just Toni and me who had the potential to dump our emotional baggage at our mother's feet down the line – she'd raised her siblings with their own hang-ups and grievances. I'm not sure I'd be issuing my *mea culpa* either.

'That was the only time I disagreed with your grand-father, by the way,' she said, almost inaudibly. 'He should have said something.'

She was quiet the rest of the day.

★ 'This Be the Verse', Philip Larkin (1971).

6

Flegs

One of my earliest assignments on my journalism course was to write an in-depth feature, tackling an unfamiliar subject area. I'd read an article that said working-class Protestant boys in Northern Ireland had been left behind by the peace process and thought it was high time I educated myself on life across the divide. I got in touch with a Protestant community worker in east Belfast and after emailing back and forth, we agreed to meet the next time I was home. He suggested he bring along some of 'the boys', who might be able to shed light on the challenges facing young loyalists in a (putatively) post-conflict society.

Mummy wasn't convinced when I informed her of my plan.

'Who are the boys, exactly? Do they know you're a Catholic?'

(I didn't tell them I wasn't Protestant until after I'd written the article, worried they wouldn't talk to me. A rookie error. They were fine about it, as the feature wasn't going to be published, but I regret not being open with them from the beginning.)

We met at a well-known tea and coffee shop a short walk from my parents' house. It seemed an unusual choice of venue for a group of hardened loyalists. In the window of the café was a laminated article about the role of caffeine in reducing the risk of Alzheimer's. I was certain the boys would stick out among the blue rinses, but apart from a solitary red hand of Ulster tattoo, semi-concealed beneath a blue shirt, they looked like all the other over-sixties enjoying their elevenses. Over caramel slices and mugs of tea, the men hinted at connections to paramilitaries during their active years. Now, they were all involved in conflict resolution, trying to convince young loyalists, who felt marginalised, that violence wasn't the answer to their grievances.

'You have to understand,' said Andy, a smiling man with big hands and an arthritic leg – his walking stick was perched against the wall – 'identity is all these young 'uns have. They come from seriously deprived communities, they can't get jobs, the Catholics are outperforming them at school . . . so when they feel like their Britishness is being taken away from them, they're angry. And you've got plenty of ones out there who'll exploit that anger.'

As Andy was talking, I noticed a strange figure outside, walking up and down past the window. They were wearing a headscarf pulled up over their nose, and dark sunglasses.

It was my mother. *Everything okay?* she mouthed.

I glared at her. She gave me the thumbs-up, then ducked out of sight.

It's four years later, December 2012. Mr G and I are married and Northern Ireland's loyalist community is in uproar after Belfast City Council votes to fly the Union Jack at City Hall only on designated days. You may have gathered we're partial to a 'fleg' in Northern Ireland – Union Jacks, the Irish tricolour, the Israeli and Palestinian flags, even Italy's green, white and red banner has made an appearance. On spotting the Bel paese's tricolour outside a primary school in County Tyrone, erected as part of a European integration project, loyalist activist Willie Frazer mistakes red for orange and immediately takes to social media to register his disgust – 'The junior headquarters of IRA youth, or it may as well be. I wonder do they also train the children in how to use weapons?' He's forced to apologise days later.

The decision to reduce the number of days the Union Jack flies outside City Hall is a compromise put forward by the centrist Alliance Party, after nationalists demand its removal altogether. Unionists claim the move is an attack on their cultural identity and take to the streets in protest. In my parents' neck of the woods, violence erupts. Buses are hijacked, churches petrol bombed. A man is arrested on suspicion of attempted murder of a police officer. Young people in hoodies carrying union flags hurl fireworks and masonry at armoured police Land Rovers, who retaliate by using water cannons on the protestors, an unthinkable tactic in any other British city. But then, different rules have always applied in Northern Ireland.

The protests continue for almost a year, the subject of both international condemnation and ridicule. I think back to what Andy said. 'Identity is all they have.' The majority of protestors are young people, born after the Good Friday Agreement, who see their Britishness as being diluted and fear any concession to the national-ists will lead to a united Ireland. Where will they fit then? The police and older loyalists like Andy accuse the UVF and UDA of capitalising on this fear by orchestrating the violence.

Weeks into the protests, I celebrate my first Christmas with the in-laws. Everyone wants to condole with me like there's been a death in the family.

'Your poor parents, what they must be going through,' my sister-in-law says.

'Ah, it's grand,' I reply, reaching for the potatoes. 'The protests are a ten-minute drive away from them. There was a booby trap bomb left under a policeman's car a couple of nights ago [outside the coffee shop where I met Andy and his friends] – I think it was the IRA who left it – but sure, the bomb disposal guys got to it before it went off. These roasties are amazing, by the way – did you use duck fat or goose fat?'

Observing the looks of horror around the table, I think about telling my new family that the protests will blow over. That we're not being dragged back into the darkness. Not yet. That yes, the recent violence is concerning, but there are plenty of people from both communities who are working hard to make sure we don't go back to the way things used to be. That Northern Ireland will always be the madness and the mundane. But I'm getting tired of having to explain myself.

Uncle Gerry's daughter Leanne got married two years later. I couldn't make it. By all accounts, the whole thing was a great success, Mummy informed me the next day. I was sitting cross-legged on the sofa in the living room of our flat, dissecting a pain aux raisins. It was my Sunday morning ritual – pastry and a two-hour phone chat with my mother, while Mr G took advantage of the one morning of the week I didn't wake him up to formulate a plan for the day ahead.

We had a good thing going, Mummy and me. True to her word, she backed off when I left home, didn't try to interfere, though she was always there for us. Possibly a bit too much. After Dan, before I started going out with Mr G, I was seeing a guy from Belfast. To facilitate our long-distance romance, Mummy booked us into a fancy hotel in Dublin for Valentine's Day. She drove down before he arrived to meet me for lunch and sprinkled the bed in our room with rose petals, then sped back up the M1 to Belfast in time for *Midsomer Murders*.

It was all very alternative, Leanne's wedding, said Mummy. The bride wore a 1950s-style dress and her brother Robert was man of honour. His heavy metal band played at the reception and everyone started thrashing about.

'Your Auntie Bernie says it's called "moshing".'

I took a sip of my coffee and pulled a face. I was drinking the stuff regularly these days, though still not out of pleasure. An editor I admired told me all serious journalists drink coffee. I wasn't a serious journalist, but I was going to be and wanted to make sure I was prepared for the role.

'Any other news from the wedding?' I asked.

'Your cousin Lucy is a bin hoker★ now.'

'It's called freeganism, Mum.'

(When I first left home for university, I quickly realised no one outside of Northern Ireland and the royal family call their parents 'Mummy' and 'Daddy', but it wasn't until I moved to London that I started trying the diminutive on for size. It never sounded right and, naturally, invites accusations of notions back home, so I save it for moments of exasperation with my mother.)

'Same thing. I do have something to tell you, though. It's a bit mad . . .'

She'd planned on not drinking at the wedding. The venue was miles away and she didn't want to pay for a taxi home, so volunteered to be the designated driver. Early on in the day, Uncle Gerry had told her they'd run out of ice. She'd offered to go to Lidl to pick up a couple of bags and was standing in the frozen food aisle when her phone went. It was a withheld number. Normally, she wouldn't answer, but assumed it was Gerry needing something else.

★ I don't know why, but sifting through refuse for unwanted items is as offensive to the Northern Irish as queue-jumping is to the English. Google 'Belfast bin hoker' if you don't believe me.

'Hello?' (I can imagine my mother's tone. Wary, immediately resenting the caller for intruding on her day.)

A pause. 'Annie?' An American voice.

'Speaking.'

'Annie, this is your little brother, Liam. We're all here. Your sisters, brothers, Mom! I can't believe I'm talking to ya, Annie!'

'_'

'Hello?'

My mother felt the blood drain from her hand – she realised she'd been gripping a bag of ice.

'Liam, not a great time. I'm buying ice for a family wedding.'

'Sure thing, Annie,' the caller chirped. 'Shall I give you a shout tomorrow?'

'That would be great. All the best, Liam.'

Mummy put her phone back in her coat pocket and methodically, almost mindfully, placed another six bags of ice in her trolley. She joined the queue at the checkout, humming to herself and flicking through a copy of *Radio Times* on the magazine rack. Then she turned her trolley around, wheeled over to the booze section and picked up three bottles of pinot grigio.

7

Uncle Kevin

'Do you think he's high?' Daddy whispered to my sister as Mummy took their guest's coat and showed him through to the kitchen.

Kevin had just arrived, or 'Uncle Kevin', as he invited Toni to call him after pulling her in for an embrace. Kevin started walking around the island in the middle of the room, drumming his fingers on the worktop. He really dug the worktop. He dug everything — Mummy, the house, Belfast — his energy magnified by his less effusive friend, who, either naturally inclined to introversion or couldn't get a word in edgeways, remained more or less mute for the duration of the evening.

Uncle Kevin is Mummy's biological half-brother. Not the biological half-brother who called her the day of Cousin Leanne's wedding while she was shopping for ice in Lidl. That was unexpected. For once, it was my mother who'd been caught off-guard. Daddy and Toni were moshing on the dancefloor when she walked up to them, her wine glass filled to the brim.

'I thought you weren't drinking today?' Toni shouted over the music.

'That's before I found out I have an American family and my birth mother is alive and well.'

This was not part of the plan. Mummy had turned sixty the previous year and was ready for a quieter life. Less drama, more *Columbo*. (Although, when asked what she wanted for her birthday, she requested a 'doobie', which I procured from Hil's daughter Lucy. She was unimpressed and concluded drugs were overrated, and that she'd made the right decision avoiding them thus far. Daddy and I maintain she never inhaled – we couldn't stop rolling around the floor.)

I need to go back to the day after the wedding. After filling me in on the phone that morning, Mummy got another call from Liam in the afternoon. Better prepared this time, she had a notepad and pen at the ready. Toni sat beside her on the sofa, making a record on her phone of Mummy's reaction to her first proper conversation with her long-lost sibling (if my sister's stitches from her severed cheek were deemed fit for posterity, this moment was bloody well going in the memory scrapbook too), while Daddy hovered at the doorway, unable to sit due to his 'nerves'.

Mummy's never been good at phone calls. She can't help but adopt an accusatory tone the minute she picks up, putting the fear of God into the unfortunate soul who was calling to see if she'd like her TV package updated. Now, she lets everything go to voicemail. Concerned she'd unwittingly give Liam the same treatment, Toni poked her in the side before she answered his call, as a reminder to behave herself.

'Hey sis!' Liam was as chipper as he'd been the day before. Throughout their conversation, he called her 'Annie'. Only Hil called her that, and not very often. Mummy wasn't sure if Liam had been supplied with the wrong information or perhaps he felt comfortable, in the way siblings do, to bestow a pet name on his new sister. Either way, she was prepared to go along with it. I wonder now whether becoming Annie gave my mother an out. In assuming a separate identity, she wasn't betraying her family. Annie was just another role to play.

The eldest of four – Nora, Kevin and Erin – Liam had only recently discovered he wasn't, in fact, his mother's first-born. A few weeks previously, on a visit from his home in Washington DC to Maryland, where his youngest sister Erin and their parents lived, Erin dragged him and their other siblings into her car, out of their parents' earshot. She wasted no time in telling them the secret she'd been protecting for almost a year.

'Mom had a daughter before Liam, when she lived in Ireland. She gave her up for adoption and we don't know what's happened to her.' Erin leaned against the headrest of the driver's seat and let out a long sigh.

'Can you imagine, Annie?' Liam laughed. 'We couldn't believe it. All this time, our mom hadn't said a word to anyone.'

Erin's mother Maggie had confided in her daughter when they were living in New Jersey, where the family had been raised, and swore her to secrecy as she didn't want to upset the boys. This annoyed Erin, she told Mummy later. Why should she be the one to carry the burden of Maggie's secret? Reluctantly, she agreed to keep quiet. It was a busy time. Her husband had been transferred to just outside Baltimore, in Maryland. As her parents were getting on in years and not in the best of health, they were moving with Erin and her family into a care home nearby.

'The first thing I thought when Erin told us about you, Annie, was "Magdalene laundries"*,' said Liam. 'We were so worried you might have ended up in one. I had to track you down and make sure you were okay.'

Mummy never really got to the bottom of how exactly Liam tracked her down. He called a cousin living in Maggie's hometown of Dungannon, County Tyrone, who had a contact in the local adoption agency. Two weeks after Erin told her siblings about Mummy, Liam had her number.

Raised on a farm outside Dungannon, Maggie was in her mid-twenties and unmarried when she got pregnant with my mother. The only time her father acknowledged her swelling bump was to tell her to 'get it sorted'. On Christmas Day 1953, a midwife drove Maggie and her youngest sister Íde across the border to Monaghan General Hospital. My mother was

---

* A system of orphanages, mother and baby homes, and industrial schools for 'fallen women', the Magdalene laundries were run by orders of Catholic nuns from the eighteenth to late twentieth centuries. Former inmates reported a culture of psychological, sexual and physical abuse. In 1993, a mass grave containing 155 bodies was found in the grounds of one of the laundries.

born the next day. After two weeks in hospital with Maggie, Mummy was taken to an orphanage in Portadown, County Armagh, where Maggie visited her as often as she could for six months before her daughter was transferred to Nazareth Lodge, in Belfast.

'You have to sign the papers if you can't keep her,' the reverend mother told her. 'Families aren't interested in older children. Do the right thing.'

A year later, Mummy Devlin adopted my mother.

Maggie moved to New York not long after. She worked for an ad agency on Madison Avenue, met her husband, and relocated to New Jersey to start a family. For sixty years, the only living person who knew about Mummy was Íde.

'I want you to know, Liam, I have no bad feelings towards your mother,' Mummy told him. 'I had a wonderful life, was blessed with my parents. Please tell Maggie she did the right thing by me.'

Toni put her hand to her chest. 'That's just beautiful,' she sniffed.

Mummy rolled her eyes.

Weeks later, she got another call from America. This time, it was Kevin, who lived in New York.

'Whaddayaknow, Annie, I'm going to be in town the week after next and would love to see you.'

He was heading to Northern Ireland for a Seamus Heaney festival with a friend. Did she fancy meeting up for dinner?

Mummy suggested they come to hers. It was the run-up to the Twelfth – not the best time to be out in town, and she was more comfortable with the idea of meeting on her own turf. They agreed she would pick them up outside Queen's University.

'Were you nervous?' I asked her, during her debrief the day after the Big Meet.

'Please! Of course not,' she said.

Toni tells it differently. She said Mummy took a notion to clean behind the radiators that day, chastised Daddy for not making enough spaghetti Bolognese, then left half an hour early to pick up Kevin and his friend.

'What did you think when you saw him for the first time?' I probed Mummy.

'I thought, "Christ, he's a midget like me".'

This was also my father and sister's reaction. Kevin was the double of Mummy, Toni said – and Steve Martin. If Kevin had been nervous about meeting his sister, he didn't show it. He talked non-stop, Daddy said, about Mom, Mummy, work – he was an actor, director and producer, and had made a short film, in which his whole family starred. When he found out Daddy was in advertising, he told him he had a script he'd love him to read. In between enthusing about his craft and enthusing about his new sister, Kevin kept disappearing to the toilet, leading Daddy to speculate that their guest had taken something. He and Toni took it in turns to check the bathroom each time Kevin left it, but they found nothing to confirm their suspicions and concluded that he wasn't high, he was just American.

'Man, when Erin told us she had something to tell us, I was like, give it to me straight, I'm adopted, right?'

Kevin said, mopping up his Bolognese with a piece of garlic bread.

Mummy shot Daddy a disapproving glance. *The man never makes enough food.*

'Turns out, Mom did have a secret, but it wasn't me!' he laughed, drum-rolling on the table.

There were further revelations. Kevin told them that when Erin had been clearing out her parents' attic in preparation for the move to Maryland, she found a shoebox containing her mother's birth certificate. Maggie was ten years older than her children had been led to believe. She'd doctored her passport before moving to America. *I'm fucking forty, girls!* Age neuroses was another thing that appeared to run in the family.

'Do you think Mummy liked him?' I asked Toni, after Kevin's visit.

'A lot. We all did. He was funny and easy-going. A bit mad, like, but sure so is Mummy.'

By the end of the night, brother and sister had their arms around each other, singing old Irish ballads, accompanied by Daddy on the guitar. It was 2 a.m. before their visitors left.

'So there you go,' Mummy said the next day. 'I've met Kevin, spoken to Liam, Maggie knows I've had a happy life. That's that.'

Erin was next up. First came the emails, then the calls. Would Mummy consider coming out to Maryland to meet Maggie? She'd pay for flights and put my parents up at her place. I assumed my mother would flat out refuse, but she told Erin she'd think about it. A few months later, she agreed. She would pay for her own flights and stay in a nearby hotel. I was surprised. My mother was never this relaxed. She'd always said she had no interest in meeting her biological mother.

'I'd rather go out there than have them landing on my doorstep,' Mummy said. 'You know what Americans are like. You invite them out of politeness and they take you up on it. But mainly, I'm doing it for Erin.'

'Why? You barely know the woman.'

'She needs this for her mummy. I'd be the same if it were my parents.'

That filial duty again.

I was thrilled she was going. It would be a good distraction for Mummy. Hil was being off with her, with all of us. We weren't sure what had happened. It started just before Kevin got in touch in the run-up to Hil's wedding (she and Uncle Brendan had divorced and Hil was remarrying). Somehow, Hil had got the impression Mummy wasn't going to go to the wedding if Gogi was invited. (Probably because Mummy said to Bernie, 'I'm not going to the wedding if Tony is invited.') She did go in the end, but things had been strained between the sisters ever since.

I was fed up with the drama. The fallouts and the secrets. The avoidance of difficult conversations. What would it be like to have a different family? A normal family. An *American* family. Everyone knows the yanks are straight shooters. I bet Erin and Kevin and their siblings got their shit out in the open and had a better relationship for it. And think of the holidays! We could visit them every summer and watch baseball games and eat apple pie and go kayaking on Lake Michigan.

'Allie, Lake Michigan is nowhere near Baltimore and you hate sports,' Toni said when I called to discuss Mummy's upcoming trip.

These facts were irrelevant. I needed to meet the Americans. I got off the phone and texted Mummy. *You're going nowhere without me.*

8

The Half-Bloods

The last time I went on holiday with my parents, they got drunk on the flight. This time around, we were split up, so I was spared the hilarious jokes and profound insights they felt compelled to share with their fellow passengers. The woman beside Mummy heard all about her Micky's psoriasis and how we were off to Jordan so he could benefit from the healing Dead Sea mud – and maybe take in a wee trip to Mount Nebo, where Moses saw the Promised Land. Her daddy named his Jack Russell after Moses, you know. Not that he was a religious man. They'd found Moses abandoned in the middle of the road outside Andersonstown leisure centre – it wasn't quite a basket in the Nile, but the name felt apt. Meanwhile, on discovering his travelling companion was an actor, my father whipped out his business card and told him he was an ad man, and would be more than happy to set him up with some work.

This wasn't a holiday. This was . . . duty? Business? (The business of coming face to face with your gene pool for the first time.) Anything but a session, and Mummy had demanded we remain sober and correct on the flight to Baltimore to meet the Half-Bloods, as she'd taken to calling her new American family. That wasn't going to be difficult for me. I met my parents at the airport that morning, not-so-fresh from a wedding the night before, where my friend reliably informed me I flashed the vicar and passed out in front of the reception desk at the Premier Inn we were staying at.

The flashing started at university. My friend Ruth finally managed to get me into the library, and I suppose I found the juxtaposition of books and breast amusing. Before long, it was my party piece, the half-time entertainment, though if I'm honest, I'm not sure who was entertained by it. Certainly not the vicar. I was tiring of it myself.

We'd been living in London for seven years. From the start, I felt at home in the city, understood. (Not literally – you learn to soften your vowels around the tenth time you're forced to say 'seven plus one' when reciting your phone number.) It's hard not to get caught up in the energy of the place. During the build-up to the 2012 Olympics, Londoners would smile at strangers, and I don't recall seeing anyone losing it in the super-market after their third 'unexpected item in bagging area'.

Standing in the queue at our local Tesco buying wine for an opening-ceremony party, we saw a guy in his twenties in a shirt and tie not only let a Chinese tourist take his place, he bought him a multipack of Hula Hoops. 'Here you go, mate. Welcome to London.' At a dinner party, I used the phrase 'cool Britannia 2.0' and no one took the piss. We spent our weekends at gastro pubs and antique shops, swooning over Victorian commodes. Mr G found a local artisan baker, who'd deliver a £3 sourdough loaf, fresh out of the oven, to our door every Saturday morning, keeping us informed on his experiments with various types of grains in his weekly newsletter. Mummy said we'd lost the run of ourselves.

But life was changing in subtle ways. The year after the Olympics, Prime Minister David Cameron pledged to hold an in–out referendum on Britain's membership of the European Union. It was clear he was trying to appease Eurosceptics in the Conservative Party, who'd been banging on for years about Brussels' attempts to dictate the shape of Her Majesty's bananas. Nothing would come of it, obviously, we said at yet another dinner party with all the smug assuredness of the dreaded metropolitan elite. (I had become addicted to dinner parties by this stage. Smug metropolitans can cook, though no almond polenta cake will ever come close to a mint Viennetta.) The UK was too liberal, too evolved, to make such a colossal mistake, we told ourselves. Pulling out of the EU would affect every aspect of British life. Sure, what would happen to Northern Ireland? The implications of reinstating a hard border in Ireland on the fragile peace so many had worked so hard to negotiate would be devastating. Crazy talk. We laughed it off.

Maybe it's the benefit of hindsight, but I can't help thinking there was a vague unease even then among my Irish and Northern Irish friends living in London. We all experienced the same jokes – English colleagues wisecracking about the Famine in their best bumbling Irish peasant accent. The 'it's just a bit of banter' was less offensive than the ignorance. A guy I met at a work event genuinely had no idea Ireland was partitioned, with an independent republic in the south and a region of the UK in the north. Someone even asked me if Northern Ireland was in a different time zone. And I'd lost count of the number of times I was told my Bank of Ulster notes – sterling, the same currency as the rest of the UK – were not accepted tender in England.

Admittedly, I was too caught up in an existential crisis to dwell on these grievances. That same year, I turned thirty and had plenty of millennial angst to keep me occupied. All around, friends were having babies and making financially sound decisions. My credit card was rejected buying toilet roll. My plans to become the next Christiane Amanpour/editor of *Vogue* hadn't quite panned out – I was working on *Beautiful Kitchens* magazine. But hey, everyone has to cook somewhere and that somewhere may as well be a beautiful kitchen. So really, this trip to visit the Half-Bloods was a welcome distraction from both impending political doom and the business of sorting my life out.

Unlike her daughter, Mummy was remarkably calm throughout the journey. She did her crossword, played solitaire on her iPad. There was nothing to indicate any trepidation about meeting the woman who'd given her up at birth. Unable to sit still, I started flicking through a magazine with Yer Man Jamie's face on the cover. He got more than the odd modelling job out of that reality show Nat and I saw him on all those years earlier. Bearded and biceped now, the man had become an international sex god. I last saw him on a 30-foot-tall screen in the cinema, telling his Hollywood co-star he doesn't 'make love. I fuck. Hard' and I have to say, it was kind of hot. Still, Mel and I spent the entire film squirming under her jacket. It was too weird watching someone from Belfast – someone we went to the same pubs with when we were younger, someone I shared a ski lift with, but didn't appreciate what it meant to share a ski lift with this person because it wasn't the person I wanted to be sharing a ski lift with – perform S&M acts in front of an audience of millions. Though it did get me thinking that the musical number I composed about Ryan in fifth year was oddly prescient – had I chosen to sing about whipping his friend instead.

As our flight had been delayed, the plan was to meet the Half-Bloods at Erin's house the next day. She'd arranged a barbecue for the whole family except Maggie, who we were visiting at her care home the day after that. It was late when we landed in Baltimore. But my hangover had gone and I felt buoyant as we made our way through Immigration. This joviality was not shared by the man checking my papers.

'Business or pleasure?'

'I'm here to meet my grandma!'

Death stare.

We picked up our bags and wheeled them into an empty arrivals hall, as Daddy scanned the signs for the taxi rank. Suddenly, there was a whoop to our left.

'There she is! Annie! Over here!'

'Oh Jesus, Mary and holy Saint Joseph,' Mummy said under her breath. There they were, our welcoming committee, a group as diminutive in stature as my mother, waving balloons and banners. First at the pass, Liam pulled 'big sis' in for an embrace and my mother was gone, passed around the Half-Bloods like a sacrificial lamb. There was nothing Daddy or I could do for her.

'How was your trip?'

'I hope you got some sleep on the flight?'

'It's sure good to see ya, Annie!'

'Do you see Mom in her? I see Mom!'

We said goodbye to the others in the car park, then Erin drove us to the hotel she'd booked. A pretty woman in her forties, with gold-red hair and doll-like features, she kept thanking us for coming. Mummy sat in the front seat and smiled and nodded as we joined a queue of giant SUVs bounding past billboards for KFC and gastric bands. Erin dropped us off, asked if we needed anything, and said she'd be back after breakfast. In our rooms, she'd left us baskets stuffed with treats – crisps, wine, Baltimore Orioles T-shirts and packets of Annie's fruit gums. Mummy grabbed a bottle of chardonnay and flopped on her bed.

The next day, after a breakfast of Cheerios and a vat of coffee, Erin picked us up. She lived in a quintessential, all-American, red-brick house that put me in mind of Kevin McCallister's place in *Home Alone*. A home worth defending. By the front door, overlooking an immaculate lawn, was a white wicker rocking chair with a cushion emblazoned with stars and stripes, and they had one of those free-standing post boxes you see in the movies at the end of the drive, the kind of post box that invites neighbourly interaction.

It was here, beside the post box, we uncovered the first family resemblance between Mummy and Maggie.

'Oh my God!' Nora, the eldest sister, tugged on Erin's shirt sleeve. 'Look!' She pointed at my mother's M&S fawn wedges. 'She's got Mom's feet. Annie is Maggie's identical foot twin!'

Erin and her ten-year-old daughter Amy leaned down to get a closer look. 'No way! They're Grandma's feet!' Amy squealed in delight.

Mummy grimaced. For years, we've teased her mercilessly about her feet. They're more like golf clubs, really. Her greatest pleasure is a foot rub; however, her lack of podiatry maintenance does little to encourage the offer of one.

After a tour of the house, drinks were poured. The Half-Bloods were easy company. Warm and generous. On a blackboard in the kitchen, someone had written 'Welcome, Annie, Micky, Alix and everyone. Love you all'. Amy, a sweet girl and straight-A student, showed me around her palatial bedroom and I felt an immediate affinity with Harrison, Erin's middle son, a fourteen-year-old in oversized shorts with train tracks, thick eyebrows and an afro. It was a bold look for an Irish American, but he owned it, proudly introducing me to his favourite item of clothing, a navy sweatshirt that said 'Afro Swag'. He reminded me of my teenage self, before my Isaac Hanson years, when I, too, believed

I had swag in abundance, fearlessly rocking up to school in my patchwork bell skirt, unfazed by the Adidas button-ups around me. *Stay special, Harrison*, I urged my cousin, without words, because I sensed we didn't need them, that my cousin and I might be telepathically connected.

I liked them all. Nora, ebullient, almost childlike in manner. Liam, Maggie's softly spoken first-born, who used to be a Wall Street hot-shot but decided to 'stick it to the man' and is now a stretch therapist in Washington. He had beef with the sugar industry and wouldn't touch the cake Erin had bought for dessert. Instead, he and his girlfriend Belinda, an ex-Buddhist nun, offered us homemade ice cream, sweetened with stevia. It was not a crowd pleaser. Kevin arrived last, journeying up from Brooklyn that morning. He made a beeline for Mummy. Daddy and Toni were right – the man was Mummy in Steve Martin's skin. We sat up late in the back garden, drinking and singing Irish songs, everyone wanting to please my mother. She'd eased into the day, enjoying the attention, and I remember thinking how long it had been since I'd seen anyone make a fuss of her.

The next day was the big meet with Maggie. It was all very cloak and dagger, Liam taking charge and instructing everyone to arrive at different times. He would go first and break the news to their father that his wife had a daughter sixty years ago, who was currently en route to meet her.

'Are you sure you want to tell him?' Mummy asked Liam.

Maggie's husband had dementia and Mummy didn't want her presence to upset him.

'He needs to know,' Liam insisted, who took his dad out for a McDonald's while the reunion took place.

Maggie and her husband lived in a bungalow on a quiet suburban street, more a house than a care home. The other residents must have been in their rooms, because, apart from Kevin, Nora and Erin, there was only one person in the communal living room, which overlooked a dense wood. Maggie sat on a floral-patterned sofa, a black handbag on her lap. She wore a pink top that clashed with dyed red hair.

'Mom?' Erin sat beside her mother and took her hand. 'Mom, Annie's here.'

Maggie looked up at my mother and nodded. 'So you're the one.'

Mummy smiled. 'I'm the one.' She sat down beside her, five sets of eyes devouring the picture.

Kevin was filming on his phone. A sniff next to me. Nora passed Erin the box of Kleenex primed on the coffee table, tears pooling in her eyes. This started me off, which started Daddy off. Within three minutes, everyone in the room was crying except Mummy and Maggie.

It wasn't so much a reunion as a performance, mother and daughter all too aware of their audience. We commented on the similarities between the two women – the same broad nose and thin lips, the shared turn of phrase. Maggie's manicure – a set of hot-pink, shiny nails on pale fingers – popped against Mummy's blood-red polish. My mother's nails have always been her one concession to personal grooming. Someone produced two mugs of tea and Maggie and Mummy posed for pictures, making jokes and playing to the crowd.

Later, I asked Mummy what she made of the experience.

'Maggie and I were the only two realists in the room,' she told me.

She went back to see Maggie alone the next day.

Maggie told her she'd prayed for Mummy every day for sixty years.

'I wanted to call you Annie, you know. After Saint Anne. But the church wouldn't let me. The priest said I couldn't name a "child of sin" after Our Lady's mother.'

My mother saw the resemblance. She recognised, in Maggie, the stubbornness of her own character – 'thran', Mummy called it. 'You had to be tough to do what she did. To give birth on your own and start a new life on the other side of the world.'

I think my mother admired Maggie's bravery and was happy she was able to put the older woman's mind at rest, to tell Maggie in person that she'd been 'blessed' with the life she's had. Friends I've spoken to about our trip to Baltimore find it hard to believe Mummy wasn't affected by meeting her birth mother, that she didn't break down from the emotion of it all. But being adopted was never an issue for my mother. She never felt like a piece of her was missing, or grappled with her identity. She's always been the full jigsaw puzzle, her sense of self absolute. She agreed to meet Maggie not because she wouldn't be complete if she hadn't, but because she felt it was the right thing to do.

We drove back to the city after that to take in the sights. I didn't know much about Baltimore. Only that it was where Meg Ryan came from in *Sleepless in Seattle* and that *The Wire* was set there. But did you know, Baltimore was also home to the world's first umbrella factory and dental school? We had another first that evening – the Half-Bloods took us to a baseball game at Oriole Park, where we waved orange foam fingers and had hot dogs and beer, and Kevin kept hugging Mummy and saying how happy he was to have her in the family. It was hugs all round when we parted ways – we'd planned on spending our last day in Baltimore, just the three of us.

Even though Kevin was driving back to New York that night, I sensed he didn't consider this the end. 'I'll see you guys real soon,' he said, with actorly intensity.

We walked Baltimore's streets the next day, stopping for blue crabs at Inner Harbor and banana cream pie in Canton. All day, I couldn't shake the sense we were being followed.

'I have the same feeling,' said Daddy, taking a furtive sip of his pint.

We were in the James Joyce pub. Mummy had just ordered that most traditional of dishes, Irish new potato nachos. 'What are you two talking about?' she said. 'Who'd be following us?'

'I could have sworn I saw Kevin earlier,' I replied, looking around.

'Kevin's in Brooklyn. He drove back last night.'

'What if he didn't go back?' Daddy whispered. 'What if he's been tailing us all day?'

'Catch yerself on, Micky,' Mummy said. 'You've been watching too much *CSI*.'

We nipped back to the hotel to get changed, then straight out again, into the warm April air. Daddy kept getting lost on our way to the steakhouse he'd booked for dinner. After the third wrong turn, we doubled back on ourselves, walking straight into Kevin as we turned the corner. Wearing the same check shirt he had on at the baseball game and dark sunglasses, he was wheeling a suitcase behind him.

'What about ya, Kevin?' said Mummy, swallowing her surprise at seeing him. 'We thought you'd gone back to New York.'

'Hey guys!' Kevin pushed his sunglasses on top of his head. 'I thought I'd hang out in the city a while longer in case you needed me.'

Daddy elbowed Mummy in an I-told-you-so kind of way. 'Have you been following us today? I could have sworn we saw you a couple of times,' he said.

'I sure was!'

'Oh.'

It was clear where I got the stalking gene.

'Er, are you staying in our hotel?' Daddy asked.

'No, I slept in my car last night. But it's all good – it's super comfortable.'

Daddy and I looked at Mummy for guidance.

She rolled her eyes and slipped her arm through Kevin's. 'Let's go have dinner.'

Four steaks, seven bottles of wine, and a karaoke performance of 'Gettin' Jiggy Wit It' later – during which my parents proclaimed their minds were blown by my rapping prowess and that I had to apply for *Britain's* – or *Ireland's* – *Got Talent* (it's never simple, is it?) the minute we got back, only to reassess this opinion the following morning on watching the video Daddy took – we staggered back to the hotel. Daddy checked Kevin into a room and carried him to bed. Didn't I tell you Americans can't hold their drink?

9

Homecoming

Mr G: *You have a grandson! Rough ride, but mum and baby doing fine.*

Mummy: *Thank God and his blessed mother! Can we pop round quickly? We're in the hotel across the road.*

Mr G: *What?? When did you arrive in London? It's 5 a.m. I don't think the hospital will let you in . . .*

Mummy: *We'll see about that.*

Ten minutes later, my mother is cradling her grandchild, Daddy looking on, finding it all 'a wee bit emotional'. Mummy doesn't even tell him to catch himself on.

At every stage of a child's early development there are causes for celebration – the first steps and smiles, yes, but also quieter moments that matter, like the subtle changes in the colour of their eyes. From a distance, my mother's eyes are brown, but up close they're an unusual mix of brown–green, a streak of grey cutting through the irises. Was that grey streak there when she was born? Or did her eyes change in the first few months of her life? Who was there to notice?

By the time my son was almost two, the age Mummy was when she was adopted, he seemed like this half-grown thing, certain of the ways of the world and the people around him. He knew books were more enjoyable when chewed, and that I would protect him from sea monsters under the bed. Looking at him one day, this little person with so much awareness, I wondered if anyone checked for sea monsters under my mother's bed. I get it now, the extended breastfeeding, the insistence on home births, the fanaticism over the health of our teeth – Mummy wanted to give us the start in life she never had.

A few months after our son was born, we decided to move to France. Mainly for the cheese, but it felt like the right time to leave London. Much as we loved the city, it began to lose its sparkle for us around the time Britain told the world it no longer wanted to be part of the EU. That sense of togetherness that was in the air during the Olympics had gone, and you'd have been hard pushed to find anyone buying Hula Hoops for a stranger in the weeks and months following the Brexit referendum. It wasn't that I couldn't understand why people would want to quit the EU, and it wasn't even the vicious mud-slinging that got to me – I was well used to division, and both sides played dirty in this war.

It was the fact that no one had considered Northern Ireland in the equation. I remember the day the Good Friday Agreement was signed. Mummy got up early and went to the bakery for hot cross buns, like she did every Good Friday. We had them – toasted, thick with butter and raspberry jam – at the kitchen table, the TV on all day as we waited for news from the negotiations, the result of 700 days of talks. At 3 p.m. she nipped out to St Agnes's to do the stations of the cross, and just before 6 p.m. British prime minister Tony Blair and Taoiseach Bertie Ahern walked out the doors of Stormont and announced a new future for Northern Ireland, a future without violence, a future where you could choose to be British or Irish, or both.

Contemplating a return to a physical border all these years later showed a casual disdain for Northern Ireland on the part of lawmakers, and how little our English compatriots knew about our corner of the world.

Now, we had a secretary of state, Karen Bradley, who admitted she was ignorant of the politics in Northern Ireland, that before taking on the job, she wasn't aware nationalists didn't vote for unionists and vice versa, and was 'slightly scared' of the place. And when the British government reluctantly joined forces with Northern Ireland's ruling party, the DUP, to get back into power, only then did many English people realise that gay and women's rights in the region were devolved. What baffled me most was the narrative of freedom pushed by many who wanted to leave the EU. 'Today we celebrate our Independence Day!' Brexiteers cried the day of the referendum result. I objected to this, not least because *Independence Day* is celluloid gold and no one can pull off presidential gravitas like Bill Pullman. But also, throughout history, Britain has been the coloniser, not the colonised. I don't recall seeing any foreign armies on London's streets.

So I'd a lot to chew over when Mr G and I went to a barbecue at a friend's house. I got chatting to a girl in the queue for food, after admiring her dress.

'Oh you're from Northern Ireland?' she said, on hearing my accent, spooning tabbouleh onto her plate. She told me her family had lived there briefly in the eighties – her father had been an officer in the Army. 'God, I hated the place. The people were *awful*. So rude and unwelcoming. I'll never go back there.'

There was a time I'd make excuses for her lack of sensitivity. She didn't realise that for many in Northern Ireland, her father and his peers weren't our saviours – they were our oppressors. And I imagine living in a place where you're made to feel unwelcome can be tough when you're a kid. I have lots of English friends. Sharp, thoughtful, culturally aware people. Yet they'll be the first to admit a gap in their knowledge of Irish history, of their own history. Because Britain's colonial past isn't taught in the UK. Ireland barely gets a mention. I see now that ignorance is a choice. For years, I chose to be ignorant about where I come from. I was wrong.

A third of people in the UK believe Britain's colonies were better off for being part of the empire.* I once met a guy who said India should be grateful to Britain for its railways. Would this nostalgia be as pervasive if the truth about the UK's imperialist history, about its role in slavery, were taught in British schools?

---

* According to a 2020 YouGov poll.

I get the reticence to go there. Obsessing over the way things were hinders progress. But is the world really any better off now? This is the time to be having these uncomfortable conversations, because there's no moving forward without them.

There's an old saying: the Irish never forget, the English never remember. The thing is, in order to forget, you need to remember – and to acknowledge past hurts. When Queen Elizabeth II came to the Republic of Ireland for an historic visit in 2011, Anglo-Irish relations were at an all-time high. She talked about the importance of 'being able to bow to the past, but not be bound by it'. She's alright, the queen.

I was quiet on the Tube ride home after my conversation with the girl at the party.

'What's on your mind?' said Mr G.

'I think I'm ready to leave London.'

We moved in with my parents for a few months in order to save for France, an unexpected development. In our mid-thirties and with a baby of our own, we hadn't planned on being part of the so-called 'boomerang generation', back with mum and dad after fleeing the nest.

Fortunately, I found my hometown a very different place to the one I'd left behind. On discovering a fantastic coffee shop near their house, with its white-washed brick and bearded baristas, I praised the owner on the quality of his java. We'd just moved back from London, you see, and were concerned we might never drink a decent flat white again.

'Three fifty,' said the man gruffly. *Ouch. London prices too.*

Outside, Mr G shook his head.

'What?' I asked.

'You're a scunderation, that's what.' (After fourteen years together, finally he was picking up the local lingo.)

Mel had a similarly 'notion-y' moment when she moved back to Belfast for a couple of months a few years ago and bemoaned the dearth of sushi joints. 'I mean, I can get a Belfast bap anywhere, but I could murder some sashimi.'

Luckily, neither of us have ever gone too far down the Path of Arsehole – the other girls wouldn't let us away with it.

There are plenty of sushi joints now. And decent flat whites. The city has been a destination for a while. I just never bothered to leave the area on my visits home to see how much things had changed. I think, in essence, though, Belfast is as it's always been – warm, welcoming, loyal, a survivor. I know that won't make much sense to those on the outside. But it's true. There's something special about the people I grew up with.

And yet . . . I could never move back to Belfast permanently. Too much hasn't changed. Like our government. Power sharing collapsed in 2017. It was three years before Sinn Féin and the DUP sat around a table once again, negotiations only picking up after the murder of journalist Lyra McKee, shot dead by dissident republicans during riots in Derry. At her funeral, the priest observed rival politicians sitting side by side and asked, 'Why in God's name does it take the death of a twenty-nine-year-old woman with her whole life in front of her' to bring them together.

Lyra's death made me angry. It made a lot of people angry. I know now it's okay to be angry, that there's a legitimacy to my anger, that if we're angry – in the right way – Northern Ireland might get the politicians it deserves. Lyra was part of a generation increasingly willing to prioritise healthcare, jobs and LGBTQ+ rights over tribalism, and that makes me hopeful for my city's future.

As for me, I've realised identity isn't something that can be foisted on you at birth, your sense of self reduced to a flag. It's a fluid structure, layers built and dismantled over the years – it's the people who raised you, the ones you surround yourself with, the books you read and the choices you make. I'd say I'm Irish first, then Northern Irish. Some days, it's the other way around. I'm a writer. A mother. A European. I'm 60 per cent sourdough, 40 per cent Belfast bap (okay, 70 per cent sourdough). I guess I'm a little bit baguette now too. I'm all my drunken nights in the Cres dancing to 'Superstar' with the girls. I'm the guilt the time our Toni fell through the roof. I'm a St Dominic's girl and eighteen years of novenas. I'm the 'Hands off my melons' top. I'm Mr G's love. Like I said, we're a complicated bunch, and that's okay. I've stopped trying to explain myself – my family, Northern Ireland. We just are. We're just us. *Never explain, never apologise.* It's time I took a leaf out of Mummy Devlin's book.

Nat and I were on our way to Niamh's for dinner one early-spring evening in 2016 when she told me she'd heard through a friend of her dad's that Gogi was going into hospital for tests. I told Mummy, and we agreed not to do anything. We had no information. They were just tests. Nothing conclusive. And none of Mummy's siblings had said anything to her. Best leave it than risk opening old wounds.

A year later, I was on Regent Street, five months pregnant and carrying the bulk of the baby in my backside, trying to find an outfit for a wedding that weekend that concealed this unfortunate redistribution of weight. I was trying on a blue dress in the changing room when Nat called. She told me Gogi had been given days to live.

'I know you guys aren't speaking and I wasn't sure if I should say anything, but I'd want to know if it were me.'

I sat down on the bench in my cubicle. 'Thanks, man. You did the right thing. Nat? What's wrong with him?'

'Throat cancer.'

I didn't know what to do. My parents were in Thailand on a detox deal they'd found in the paper. Mummy seemed happier than she'd been in a long time. The year after my wedding, Moira died. Mummy visited her in the hospital every day. She painted her nails, gave her a foot massage, tried to keep her friend's spirits up. She doesn't talk about the end much. My mother's no stranger to death, but I know losing Moira took its toll. She stopped going to the novena after that.

The day after Nat told me about Gogi, I spoke to Mummy. The self-administered colonics were paying off and their reiki master had told her she had the purest energy he'd ever seen. Daddy was sulking because he told him he saw deep guilt and shame in his aura.

I texted Toni to ask her to call me back when she got up – it was late in Sydney (my sister moved to Australia a few years ago) – then dialled Bernie's number. She had no idea Gogi was sick and asked me if I was going to tell Mummy. I thought about not saying anything. Letting her have her holiday and her pure energy, and waiting until she got back to share the news. I suspected she wouldn't fly home for the funeral anyway. Mummy had made peace with her relationship with Gogi a long time ago.

I didn't sleep that night, and for the first time in weeks, it wasn't the baby keeping me awake. Do I tell Mummy now or wait? *Be kind or tell the truth?* In the end, I decided she needed to know. I wondered if that was a cop-out. If I didn't want the responsibility of keeping a secret from my mother on my shoulders.

Either way, she was glad I'd told her. She said she'd been preparing for the call. Gogi was seventy-two, and until he quit smoking a decade earlier, had a forty-a-day habit. She knew this day would come and had time to think about what she would do. And that was to do nothing.

I didn't go to the funeral either. But I did call Gogi's wife Penny. To condole with her? To try to speak to Gogi? And if so, for whose benefit? His? Mine? I'm still not sure. He lost consciousness that morning, Penny told me, but he was comfortable, at peace. He was hurt, 'so hurt', by everything that went down between us.

Join the club. I didn't blame Penny for the hint of accusation in her tone. Her husband was dying upstairs, and as far as she was aware, his family had abandoned him. She didn't know what really happened. To be honest, I don't know what really happened. I do know that I loved my uncle, and that my childhood was richer for having him in it.

Mummy and John stopped speaking after Gogi died. When she got back from Thailand, she called John. Their conversation was strained. John seemed to think his sister knew Gogi had been sick and didn't tell the rest of them. More secrets. They had no contact for two years, until John called out of the blue last March. He and Liz were heading to Belfast that weekend. Could they see her on the Sunday? Mummy said to come round for lunch. John brought wine and a bouquet of flowers; Daddy made salmon. No one mentioned Gogi. Before they left, John asked Mummy if they were okay, and Liz said she was sorry about everything that had gone down between them.

Mummy put an arm around each of them. 'You're here now.'

It was Mother's Day.

To paraphrase Uncle Gerry, not everything's a happy fuckin' ever after. Hil and Mummy still aren't talking. I haven't seen my aunt since her wedding six years ago. Maybe there were too many secrets for Hil. Maybe the family dynamic was too complex to endure. Maybe it just comes down to personality. The only way to resolve conflict is to accept differences, and I don't think Mummy and Hil ever really accepted each other's differences.

I miss Hil sometimes, her loud laugh, her straight-talking. I miss what my family used to be, mad and dysfunctional as it was. But my mother seems happier without the undercurrent of tension that was always there between her and her sister, even when things were good. I hope Hil is happier too. Before Gogi died and when everyone was still on speaking terms, I made a book for Mummy's sixtieth birthday and asked her siblings to share stories about their sister. They all said the same thing: that she was the glue who kept them all together. Maybe Mummy got tired of being the glue.

Recently, government ministers raised the idea of a Mandela-style truth and reconciliation commission for Northern Ireland as a way to deal with the legacy of the Troubles. Openness and transparency – we're told these are the things that help build bridges. I hope I'll be as honest as possible with my children and prepared for difficult conversations when they arise. Because on the whole, I think the truth is the best thing. (I can hear Sister Frances now. *Veritas, girls!*)

Which is easy for me to say. I've never had secrets my parents asked me to keep or identities to protect. I haven't had to clean a dead man's blood off a barstool then send my kids off to school like nothing happened. I haven't had to worry about how to explain to my children why someone would blow up a street full of innocent Saturday shoppers or gun down punters at a Halloween party in a pub. *Whatever you say, say nothing.* I don't know what choices I would have made had I been in my mother's shoes, but I do know she has more strength in those club toes of hers than anyone

I've met. And that's why I'll always keep boomeranging back to her. Because she's home. And I'm proud of where I came from.

I really need to start packing, but I'm distracted by a memory box I've unearthed at the bottom of my old wardrobe. There's a note from Nat scribbled during one of our detentions, the wrapper from the Mars Dan melted that Valentine's Day and a photo of Toni, Daddy Devlin and me, getting ready for one of our Christmas Eve walks with the dogs. I bring it downstairs to show Mummy. She's at the kitchen table, FaceTiming Toni, *Father Brown* (the crime-solving priest) on in the background. My son is sitting on her knee.

'Come and say hello to your sister,' she calls.

My son looks confused. 'That's Auntie Toni,' he corrects Mummy, pointing at the screen with a pudgy finger.

'Yes, Toni is your mummy's sister,' my mother explains. 'And I have two sisters. Actually, I have six sisters.'

'Four,' I say, taking a seat beside her and waving at Toni. 'Hil, Bernie, Erin and Nora.'

'There's the ones you don't know about yet.'

'What do mean?' says Toni, leaning a tanned face into the camera.

'She's joking. You're joking, right?' I turn to my mother. 'Please tell me you don't have any more family members in the closet.'

My mother smiles and taps her nose with her index finger.

'That's for the next book, baby.'

Afterword

May 2020

Full disclosure – I had no intention of writing about growing up in Belfast, in Belfast. There's this dreamy early-morning light that fills the hallway of our house in France, the space containing nothing but a standard lamp that belonged to Mummy Devlin and my grandfather's rolltop writing desk. It would be here, I told anyone who cared to listen – on the same slab of mahogany Daddy Devlin used to pore over the latest issue of *Chess* magazine, an exquisitely crafted macaron in front of me, an overpriced scented candle on the go – I would write my book.

Absolute notions, of course.

So far, 2020 has had little interest in my grand plans, or anyone else's, for that matter. The majority of these pages were written in the office above my parents' garage. There are no macarons, only coconut fingers from The Golden Crumb down the road (to be fair, you'd be hard pushed to find a superior coconut finger in all of east Belfast). Instead of the rising sun gently stirring me into action, I've been spending my days under a fluorescent strip light, listening to Mr G pound on his keyboard with all the grace of a baby elephant. He says he'd rather take his chances with the coronavirus than endure another minute of me narrating every action of my working day – 'I'm just going to hit "send" on this wee email here, then have a pee'. As for a scented candle, I asked Mummy if she had one lying around. I was feeling uninspired and needed to create the necessary writerly ambiance. She gave me a thirtieth anniversary Clonard novena candle and told me to ask Our Lady for inspiration and give her head peace.

We've been staying with my parents since February. Midway through a month-long trip to Ireland, so the boys could spend time with both sets of grandparents (our second son was born a few months after we moved to France), Covid-19 sent the world into lockdown. Our flight back has been cancelled three times and we've no idea when we'll get home.

Adjusting to our new multigenerational set-up hasn't been the easiest ride. Our eldest has taken to barging in on Daddy on the toilet to applaud him on attending to his business, while I've been less than thrilled at the amount of screen-time he's getting on my mother's watch – last week, he asked me to turn on *Diagnosis: Murder*.

Mr G maintains *he's* suffered the greatest hardship. Not long after we arrived, the toddler started crying in the middle of the night. Unaware Mr G was already in the room with him, Mummy ran in to comfort her grandson. 'Where's my beautiful big boy?' she cooed, feeling her way in the dark up an unexpectedly sturdy leg. On realising she'd just manhandled her son-in-law, she fled the room. Breakfast the next morning was an unusually quiet affair.

In truth, we know how lucky we are. To be here with family, attempting to navigate the uncertainty together. Australia has closed its borders to try to contain the virus and we don't know when we'll see Toni again. My parents have been absolute heroes, taking care of the boys while we work – a privilege I don't take for granted – and for our allotted daily exercise, we've the grounds of Stormont on our doorstep. (Seat of unionist oppression or not, even Moira wouldn't have turned down a morning constitutional in nature in times like these). While the pain is real for so many and cannot be diminished, there's a reassuring simplicity to the new normal. Small joys that take the edge off the gnawing anxiety – a favourite coffee shop reopening for take-aways, rainbows scribbled in crayon and taped to every other window. And a stillness to a city that was never still.

We've managed to keep some semblance of a social life. The girls and I threw a Zoom baby shower for Mel a few weeks ago, signing on from London (Mel), Dublin (Nat) and Belfast. After a few years in Dublin, Jennifer and Sammy came back home to start a family. (Sammy is still into Jennifer, but not trance. Verse is his thing now, though he likes to keep his craft on the down low. Jennifer was on Amazon a while back and came across an anthology of poetry he'd composed.

They'd been living together for years – she had no idea when he'd found the time to write a book.) Niamh and Johnny are also here by accident, over from London to visit family. Even though Johnny's parents live a two-minute walk from mine, Niamh and I can't hang out, so have been resorting to enthusiastic mime waves over the hedge.

The five of us have been through it all together. Losing jobs, losing parents, losing babies. Now one of us is about to give birth to her first child, in a pandemic. It's funny to think there was a time when the worst of our troubles were gunmen kicking all the Catholics out of our favourite pub, leaving us with nowhere to buy cheap booze. And that wasn't even the worst of our Troubles. Twenty years later, the world around us is rumbling again, only this time, it's harder to shut out the noise.

The only person we've seen in the flesh since this all this started is Uncle Gerry. He comes and sits on a bench in the garden, keeping the mandatory two-metre distance. The man's not messing around. He was in Sainsbury's recently and a woman got too close for comfort in the fruit and veg aisle.

'You think this is a fuckin' magic shop?' he said. 'You're not gonna catch the coronavirus buying yer mangetout?'

At first, the official reaction to the virus in Northern Ireland was as you'd expect it to be – political. When the Irish taoiseach Leo Varadkar announced schools in the Republic would close a week before the UK adopted the same measures, Sinn Féin demanded

Northern Ireland follow suit, with some Catholic schools refusing to wait for Stormont to make up its mind. The DUP was less keen on a cross-border approach to tackling the pandemic, biding its time to see what call Westminster would make. Finally, there seems to be some consensus, and for the first time in a long time (devolved government in the region had been back up and running just ten months when Covid hit), Northern Ireland's leaders are working together to try to get us back to normal. Whatever that looks like. No country has a magic fix for this one, certainly not the UK or America. These were the grown-ups in the room when I was growing up, when we were the ones making the mess, kicking up a fuss. I don't think there are any grown-ups anymore.

Speaking of Americans, Erin left a voicemail for Mummy the other day to see how we were all doing. Right up until Maggie died in 2016, Mummy spoke to her birth mother every week. I think she enjoyed their conversations. 'It's my daughter,' Maggie would tell her friends in the care home whenever Mummy called. My mother didn't go to the funeral. She said she didn't feel it was necessary, and told Erin she wouldn't be flying over. Erin appeared not to get the memo – when she and her family came to visit the following year, Erin told Toni they 'put Mom on ice for a month' waiting for Mummy. We haven't seen the Half-Bloods in a while, but Mummy and Erin email and chat on the phone from time to time. Which is more than a lot of full-bloods manage. They're good people, the Americans. They'll never replace the family my mother grew up with – even with all their issues – but there's a comfort in knowing they're there, across the Atlantic.

It's one of few comforts these days.

'Do you get the feeling the world is about to end?' I ask Mummy. We're watching the news in the kitchen. Mummy's sitting at the table sewing a felt eye onto the baby snowman she's making for the Christmas family tableau. 'I mean, it feels like it's never been this bad.'

She raises a white eyebrow over her glasses. Fair point. When you've lived through the Troubles, Cuban Missile Crisis, four global recessions and Sinead O'Connor tearing up a photo of Pope John Paul II live on TV, you get used to feeling the world is about to end.

'What choice do you have?' she says. 'You can believe everything's shit and humanity's screwed, or you can choose to be hopeful.'

I see this choosing of hope in the crayon rainbows in the windows. In the local businesses that are adapting to survive and the vendors who give you a coffee when you forget your purse – 'Just drop it off next time you're passing, love'. They've made a choice to look forward, face the uncertainty, believe things will be different. Because they've done it before. Because it's what we do.

My phone pings. A photo pops up on the Belfast Girls WhatsApp – a chubby arm, the face of an exhausted, beaming mother.

I smile at Mummy. 'Mel's had a little girl.'

Acknowledgements

The Troubles with Us could never have been written without the support of family, friends and a crack team of professionals, to whom I owe a world of gratitude. A big, fat shout-out to:

Mr G, who persuaded me to pitch the idea for the book when I thought no one would be mad enough to publish a memoir about underage stalking and bombs in coffee jars; providing endless advice, pep talks, editorial suggestions and boundless patience as always. I love you.

The best editor a girl could ask for, Louise Haines, for the brilliant insights and guidance, and for making this experience so much fun.

Fellow Northern Irish gal and agent extraordinaire, Nicola Barr, who helped me hone my book proposal and believed in this project from day one. You rock.

The shit-hot production team at 4th Estate, in particular Marigold Atkey, Emma Pidsley for the wonderful cover design, and copyeditor Aonghus Meaney.

To my Belfast Girls, the best friends a girl could ask

for: thank you for letting me divulge a fraction of our many teenage humiliations. You're Superstars, every one of you.

To Ruth Patten, Lucie McInerney and the Journos: for the unwavering support, and for listening to me shite on about how writing a book is harder than birthing a human. And to everyone else who has supported the book.

The team at General Merchants East Belfast, for fuelling the writing process with flat whites, huevos rotos and good old Belfast craic – all during a pandemic.

Finally, to my family: My aunts, uncles and D-squared (you know who you are), for the madness and the memories.

I am so grateful to my father, Micky not only for his cartography skillz (see map at front), but for looking after my children while I wrote this memoir and for not telling Mummy about that time I went to the Crescent.

To my Sister, Sister, Toni, for always having my back. Your love and support means the world to me.

W & S, for being awesome. How lucky I am to be your mummy.

And to my main woman, my mother, Anne. Thank you for the unperforated teeth, your story to share – and everything else.